IMRAN

IMRAN

The autobiography of
Imran Khan
with Patrick Murphy

PELHAM BOOKS

First published in Great Britain by
Pelham Books Ltd
44 Bedford Square
London WC1B 3DU
1983

British Library Cataloguing in Publication Data

Khan, Imran
    Imran.
    1. Khan, Imran   2. Cricket players—Pakistan
    —Biography
    I. Title   II. Murphy, Patrick
    796.35'8'0924   GV915.K/

    ISBN 0–7207–1489–3

Typeset by Cambrian Typesetters, Aldershot, Hants
Printed and bound in Great Britain by Billing and Sons, Worcester

Contents

List of Illustrations

Acknowledgements

The author and publishers are grateful to the following for permission to reproduce copyright photographs: R.R. Booker nos 8 and 9; Patrick Eagar nos 12, 13, 14, 15, 18, 20, 23, 24, 25, 33; John Fairfax and Sons Ltd nos 10, 11; *Herald and Weekly Times*, Melbourne no 22; Ken Kelly nos 7, 27, 28, 29, 30, 31, 32, 34, 35; *Sports Week* no 17; Zafar Ahmed no 36.

In some instances the copyright owner is not known and it is hoped that any omissions will be excused.

1 Early Days

The game of cricket and I travelled on distinctly separate paths for the first eleven years of my life. Quite frankly, I agreed with my father that it was a boring game with too much standing around. I was good at other sports and saw nothing special about cricket, even when my mother took me to watch the West Indies in a Test Match. The sight of Wes Hall tearing in to bowl from the sightscreen certainly didn't inspire this seven-year-old. When I watched the Pakistan opener Ijaz Butt being carried off with a broken nose as the blood poured down his shirt, I was even less enthusiastic. In later years, I became more philosophical about opening batsman's injuries!

Yet I suppose it was inevitable that I should be hooked on cricket. My family background pointed me in that direction — no less than eight of my first cousins from my mother's side have played first-class cricket and two have captained Pakistan. My mother's side of the family housed the cricketers: to this day, my father remains blissfully unaware of much of the game's subtleties. One of my mother's most vivid memories of cricket stems from the days when her family lived in Jallunder before Partition; the men in the family would play cricket all day. Mother and her two sisters produced three sons who went on to lead our country — Majid Khan, Javed Burki and myself. Majid's father — Jehangir Khan — was a Cambridge Blue in the 1930s who played four times for India, and his brother Asad was also an Oxford Blue. My only uncle on my mother's side — Ahmad Raza Khan — was also a renowned first-class cricketer before Partition and his two sons followed him in playing first-class cricket. So cricket was well and truly in my blood and when my mother's family had one of their regular gatherings, the main topic of conversation was — you've guessed it.

By the time I was eleven, several things were happening to me that, in hindsight, were very significant to my cricket career. The first was our move to the Zaman Park area of Lahore. All my family who lived there played cricket to a very high standard and that tradition remains to this day. Javed Zaman was always in charge of Zaman Park's sporting activities — he was my mother's first cousin and called 'The Godfather' by us. Zaman Park was named after his father.

Zaman Park is not a very large area but it has spawned an amazing number of first-class cricketers — the big park in the middle of the area was kept busy with sports activities in general and cricket in particular and the standard was high indeed. Too high for this particular youngster. The ages would range from ten to forty and I was very much last on the list when it came to team selection. As the captains picked their sides I would stand there, crimson with embarrassment, knowing that I wasn't rated. I could hardly blame them — my bowling was more of a danger to my own fielders than to the batsmen and my attitude to fielding was, to say the least, aristocratic. As for my batting — well, a couple of balls was usually enough to defeat my headstrong swish of the bat. Clearly I wasn't totally naïve, though; after being dismissed, I'd stand my ground at the crease, throwing tantrums, pleading that I wasn't ready for the delivery, refusing to budge, anything to prolong my stay.

The histrionics never worked, I was out of my class and knew it. As a bad loser, I was tempted to escape from cricket and try my hand in other sports at which I was better; I hated the idea of playing a sport badly. The problem was that nobody of my age group seemed to want to play anything other than cricket, so I had to keep plugging away, trying to follow the cricket conversation of my family and wondering if I'd ever get to grips with the game. Luckily, help was at hand in the person of a kindly old games superintendent at my prep school. Naseer Ahmed was games superintendent at Aitchison College and I can remember vividly the day he changed my attitude to cricket when I joined prep school. I had just compiled twelve runs in a marathon innings of four balls when Naseer Ahmed came up to me and dissected my gem of an innings. He called it a slog and typical of my efforts; if I did it again, I wouldn't be in the prep school team. He said he didn't mind how long I stayed at the crease or how slowly I scored as long as I followed the two basics of batting — playing back to the ball pitched short and forward to the delivery that was pitched up. In both cases, a straight bat was essential, not the carving, flashing blade I tried to wave around with abandon. That piece of advice was a watershed in my career. From that day onwards, my batting improved dramatically and I enjoyed my cricket immensely. No longer was it a necessary evil to play cricket with my elders on Zaman Park: it now became an obsession. After school I'd play in Zaman Park and then I'd make our servants and my sisters bowl at me for hours and at sunset I'd move the game indoors, with a resulting threat to the well-being of mirrors and windows. No wonder two of our servants left to seek alternative employment — bowling till midnight wasn't on the agenda!

Around this time, I decided I was going to play for Pakistan. As simple as that. It was just a question of time, I decided. To my uncomplicated eyes, I was the best young player around and my sights were set on becoming the youngest to represent Pakistan in Tests. Majid Khan (six years my senior) was already making his mark in Tests, so why should I be any different when my call came? Such were the clear-cut issues that faced a boy of eleven from my privileged, cloistered background. I was the best batsman in my prep school team and later on in the school team I made my mark in our annual fixture with Lawrence College by top scoring.

I suppose this feeling of superiority was a natural result of being born into a privileged environment. I was aware of my good fortune very early: Pakistan is a country where class divisions are sharply drawn. My father was a brilliant engineer with a post-graduate degree from Imperial College, London, who had joined the Government service. My mother's family was even more comfortably off. The best cricket ground in Lahore belongs to the Gymkhana Club; you need money and influence to become a member there. It was dominated by my mother's family. As I improved my cricket, I was taken to the Gymkhana by Javed Burki and Majid for some net practice, a privilege denied to boys of greater talent than mine. By the time I was fourteen, I was playing club cricket for Gymkhana whenever the members decided the heat was too intense for them. I was also very lucky with my school. Aitchison College, Lahore, is our equivalent to England's Eton or Harrow; the pupils expect life to be good to them. Our school cricket team was so good that we didn't think most schools were good enough for us so we took on club sides. The facilities were marvellous and I believe the Aitchison College ground to be one of the most beautiful cricket areas I've seen. The Gymkhana ground was even prettier than the Parks at Oxford, a place I grew to love during my spell there as an undergraduate. If I hadn't been lucky enough to play cricket in my formative years on two such lovely grounds, I doubt if I would have made my name in cricket. I wonder if I would have persevered if I had to play all my cricket in Iqbal Park, where ten matches at a time could be going on, or on the matting wickets of Karachi. Most of my team-mates in the Pakistan team have had to fight hard to raise their playing standards in hostile conditions. That kind of determination stood them in good stead.

So I was lucky to be born into a comfortable background where I didn't have to worry about anything. I was also fortunate to be inspired eventually by my two illustrious cousins. At school, everyone talked to me about Javed Burki. I'd watched him score a hundred at Lahore against the touring England team and I basked in his reflected glory, especially when he did it again in that series and followed up with another century at Lord's a few months later. I took great family pride in his achievements and although I was then more talented at swimming, soccer and hockey, I suppose Javed's example subconsciously stirred my ambition. Majid was more influential on a personal level; he was at the same school as me and his batting performances were legendary. He didn't know how to defend, his timing was superb and his strokeplay dazzling. When he made a hundred and took six wickets on his first-class debut at the age of fifteen, we accepted it as the normal course of events. After all, we couldn't get him out during our matches on Zaman Park, so why should it be different for lesser mortals? When he first played for Pakistan at eighteen years of age, our only comment was that it had taken the Test selectors far too long to recognise genius. Majid was just like an elder brother to me, and remained so throughout his glittering Test career. I could ask him for anything at any time and he was always totally supportive. How many other cricketers have had the good fortune to be coached by two Test captains? Yet at the time, I took it all for granted and I just breezed through my adolescent years.

At that time, I had no ambitions at all to be a fast bowler, yet luck again helped me. When I am asked about the various influences on my fast bowling career, I always get a bemused reaction when I mention kite-flying. Lahore has a strong tradition of kite-flying that is not surpassed anywhere else in Pakistan and this winter activity toughened up my legs for fast bowling. The craze was at its peak when I was a teenager; I used to chase kites from one part of Zaman Park to the other, a distance of a mile. I would sprint, not just jog along, sometimes about a hundred sprints a day. It would often be like an obstacle course — chasing kites over walls, hedges, fields, roads and ploughed land. The season lasted for two months and I chased kites for about five years. Without realising it at the time, my legs and knees got tougher and tougher. As a result, I have never had chronic problems in an area that is often very vulnerable for a fast bowler.

I was cricket-crazy, spending the entire week waiting for Sunday's match and sitting up most of Saturday night, praying for clear skies. The monsoon weather often gave me nervous twitches! I don't know how I would have survived my early cricketing years in England! High summer in Lahore was always a marvellous time for me because the heat would drive many of the Gymkhana members away. I would stay in Lahore to play in the Wazir Ali league while my family would go to the hills. I would then get regular club cricket and shrug off the intense heat. The games started at seven in the morning and after three hours, we would stay out of the sun and resume play at four o'clock. Once I remember losing five pounds in weight in the first hour of play, only to put it back on again with liquids. Once you survived that kind of weather, playing cricket during the Pakistan first-class season in winter was easy.

With school and club cricket under my belt, I considered myself ready for the wider cricketing public by the time I was sixteen. In all modesty, I have to admit I saw myself as the next Bradman. I conceded privately that Majid might just have the edge over me in strokeplay, but I generously allowed him to be the other genius in the family. Cricketing excellence was in my blood, so who was I to argue with the fates that had so liberally sprinkled me with stardust?

I was by far the best batsman in my school and the game of cricket looked considerably easier than in those traumatic early games on Zaman Park. I had no interest at all in bowling; I would simply turn my arm over in the nets and on the rare occasions when I bowled in a game, the fielders would look at me, rather than the batsman, because the ball could easily hit them, rather than pitch on a length! No young cricketers in Pakistan hero-worshipped bowlers at that time; it was a batsman's game in my country and our heroes were men like Hanif and Mushtaq Mohammad and my two cousins, Javed and Majid. Certainly no one wanted to become a fast bowler because there was no inspiration from any top players — the Test seam attack consisted of Asif Iqbal and Niaz Ahmed (both military medium), Majid himself (medium pace) and the injury-prone Saleem Altaf. Hardly a quartet to make a boy long to bowl fast in hot weather and on slow wickets.

As I grew taller, I suddenly found I could bowl quite sharply. My physique obviously helped — I was fairly tall and strong at sixteen — and I rather enjoyed watching batsmen hop around at my short-pitched deliveries. I was very wayward and had no idea where the ball was going, so I didn't take my bowling seriously. After all, re-writing the batting record books was going to take up all my time in the near future. An occasional bowling spell was ideal for warding off boredom in the field but no more than that. All that changed one afternoon when I was sixteen.

I was summoned to the under-nineteen trials that were to choose a team to play the visiting England side. I accepted the invitation as no more than my due, even though I was three years younger than the other trialists: already I had come to terms with the fact that my colossal talent had catapulted me beyond my age group! There must have been a couple of hundred trialists in the nets that day, very few of whom were under the age of nineteen; it has been a normal feature of Pakistan cricket to hide your real age. When my turn came to bat, I strode to the net with my customary aplomb. At last the time had come when my precocious talent would be unveiled to a wider audience; I raised my collar in the approved superstar manner, tugged at my cap and took my time in marking my guard. For the occasion I had bought cricket spikes and wore them for the first time. It made a complete mess of my footwork. I faced no more than a dozen balls before one of the selectors shouted 'Next please!' and I had to vacate the net. I consoled myself with the thought that I had obviously shown enough promise to convince the selectors of my worth in just a few minutes — time was pressing on, after all, and they needed a longer look at the fringe candidates. Conveniently I ignored the fact that six of the dozen deliveries had completely beaten me. As I stood watching the other trialists in the nets, reality slowly seeped into my brain: I was a reject. The selectors were ignoring me — the prodigy.

After a time, I was told to go in a net and bowl. After my second delivery, the chairman of the selectors stopped the whole proceedings and singled me out for special attention. I thought that he was going to nominate me as the worst bowler at the trial and reward me with another batting spell, but no, he told me to bowl another delivery and made everyone watch. To my utter astonishment, he pronounced mine the ideal fast bowler's action and told the assembled group that I was a promising opening bowler. I was selected for the under-nineteen match as opening bowler and — the unkindest cut of all — tail end batsman. What was on the selectors' minds?

They must have asked themselves that question when I bowled for Lahore under-nineteen against England under-nineteen. Four overs, four maidens may sound an impressive start to a representative career, but the batsmen didn't lay a bat on a single delivery of those four overs because they couldn't get anywhere near them. It was the first time I'd ever opened the bowling in a match and I was truly embarrassed. Wasim Raja, my captain and subsequent colleague in the Test side, did the decent thing and took me off. It was beginning to dawn on me that cricket wasn't as easy as I thought. How could they see me as a bowler who could bat a little? Surely it was the other way round? Well the selectors' judgement was vindicated in the second innings when I managed to still my nerves and took 3 for 7, bowling fairly fast and surprising myself. I discovered the bouncer during that innings and proceeded to bowl it far too frequently; I loved seeing batsmen protect themselves, rather than their stumps and even rough treatment from good hookers failed to knock the fondness for bouncers out of my system. Tactical sense in bowling wasn't important since I saw it to be a transitory thing as my real passion was batting.

I made my debut in first-class cricket for Lahore against Sargodha. I was sixteen-and-a-half, a year older than Majid when he made his debut. Gradually it was dawning on me that there was a huge gap between the Majids and the Imrans: Wasim Raja was the same age as me, but he looked astonishingly mature as a batsman, playing shots I couldn't possibly achieve. I realised that my first-class debut was not a reward for outstanding play, more a recognition that there were no fast bowlers around, and that the top Lahore players had left to join the PIA side, leaving many vacancies. There was also another reason for my selection — nepotism. The chairman of selectors was my uncle, the side was captained by my cousin Hammayun Zaman and Javed Zaman was also in the team. Truly a family affair; why else would I be picked as both opening bowler and opening batsman? My perform- ance hardly matched that of Majid on his debut — two wickets and 32 runs. To make matters worse, I overslept and missed the start of our second innings! It had rained heavily and I thought the game would not start on time —

it did and someone else stood in for me. When I batted, I was run out and we lost the match.

For a time things got even worse. I pulled a back muscle through trying to bowl too fast and for a year I couldn't bowl properly. I was bowling too fast for my body and it just couldn't take the strain. Eventually, I started on a course of training that toughened up my back. Since then I have had little trouble in that area. I was frustrated at being unable to bowl, but it would have been far worse if I'd missed out on batting. In my eyes I was still a batsman who could bowl a bit if necessary, rather than the other way round. By the time my back injury had cleared up, I was seventeen-and-a-half and a totally different bowler — my stock ball was now the inswinger and I had lost the ability to move the ball away from the bat. Without realising it, I had become more open-chested in trying to take the strain off my back. All I could do was bowl huge inswingers that might go anywhere; my action was very awkward and I'd be leaning back so much that I wasn't looking at the batsman or his stumps. Javed Burki told me that I wouldn't last very long as a fast bowler because of my unnatural action and I accepted that. Javed asked Billy Ibadulla — a Test batsman, respected coach and player with Warwickshire — to take a look at me and I well remember Billy's advice: 'You've got a really bad action — but don't change it.' Perhaps Billy was hinting at something that I learned later in my career — that you don't need a beautiful action like Dennis Lillee's to be a top fast bowler. Today it really amuses me when people compliment me on my bowling action. If only they could have seen what it was like a few years ago!

In the short term, my huge inswingers brought me a harvest of easy wickets. The average club cricketer in Pakistan doesn't know much about the forward defensive stroke, preferring to play across the line with the hook, the pull and the cut; as a result, I bowled many batsmen through bat and pad on the occasions when I managed to harness the swing. During the 1970–71 first-class season, I took more wickets than anyone except Sarfraz Nawaz, the man with whom I would share the new ball for Pakistan over the next decade. Although I often struggled with my action and my line, I still managed to click and get it all right on occasions and those often coincided with vital moments in big matches. I had inherited an aggressive, competitive attitude to cricket from the Zaman Park games, so that I wasn't overawed by tense moments in the matches. My captain in the Lahore side was usually my cousin, Javed Burki, and he handled me very well indeed; he kept me away from the good batsmen in case my confidence was destroyed and he encouraged me to bowl fast when he thought the situation was right.

Due to Javed's shrewd captaincy, I managed to impress the selectors sufficiently to be picked for the tour to England in 1971. I hadn't lost my cockiness completely and chose to ignore the fact that I had played less than ten first-class matches. Deep down, I knew that I was only picked because there were no other fast bowlers around and that a boy of just eighteen couldn't expect to take English cricket by storm. I also realised that my education must not be ignored, a fact that worried my parents. I promised them that my studies wouldn't suffer and that I would pick up the academic threads once the tour was over. For the moment the lure of Test cricket was the dominant thought in my mind: I had told myself that I was going to play for my country. My only regret was that it had taken such a long time for me to do so.

2 A Rude Awakening

The 1971 Pakistani tour party to England contained one player who must surely rank as the rawest, most conceited cricketer ever to represent his country. Me. As far as I was concerned, I was going to be the star of that trip, my entry into the Test arena was overdue. I would day-dream about the hundreds I'd score off bowlers who had just regained the Ashes in Australia and I'd settle for nothing less than five wickets each innings. On the isolated occasions that things didn't go quite according to plan, I could always turn to Majid for advice: although he was now at Cambridge, he would be available for the Tests, ready to guide me along the slopes to greatness. In vain did Majid warn me about the tour: he insisted that it was part of my cricket education, that I would return a better player, but unlikely to figure prominently during the trip. My mind was made up. I was ready for the world. I suppose most cricketers at some stage do such fantasising.

For some reason, most of the tour party didn't share my optimism, either about my prowess or about the team's prospects. Many of them kept going on about the tactical skills of the England captain, Ray Illingworth, and the batsmanship of men like Geoff Boycott, John Edrich, Colin Cowdrey and Basil D'Oliveira — not to mention the fearsome fast bowling of John Snow. The experienced ones in our camp talked at length about the way the ball swings and seams in England; they were phrases that I just didn't understand. Someone said that Alan Ward, one of England's opening bowlers, was faster than Wes Hall, and some of the juniors like Talat Ali wondered if we would see the ball at all once it left his hand. They would say that the fielding in England was so good that if you nicked the ball, there was no point in looking round to see if the catch had been taken. Our bowlers were told by the experienced hands that we would do well just to beat the bat. Of course all this was just a greater challenge for me.

My first stint in the nets made me realise that things were going to be a little different from my preconceptions. I strolled up in my new, immaculate kit, wearing my brand-new boots and proceeded to ease into my bowling. My first delivery missed Aftab Gul's nose by a matter of inches. Unfortunately he was batting in the adjoining net. After a host of apologies from me and some colourful Punjabi abuse from the shattered batsman, I prepared for my second delivery on English soil. It was no trouble to the batsman, but perturbed a spectator. It hit him on the head. He beat a hasty retreat from the side of the net that he'd deemed a safe place to watch us. By now it had dawned on even my over-confident mind that something was wrong. I realise now that I was bothered by the difference between the hard grounds of Pakistan and the soft, damp turf of Lord's, with the result that I couldn't keep a proper foothold — despite the new spikes. I was sent into a net on my own to sort myself out. In just a few deliveries, I had brought the entire net practice to a standstill.

For a long time, I couldn't get the ball anywhere near the stumps; when I managed to do that, I kept over-stepping the crease. Eventually I just ambled up to the crease and more or less stopped in my tracks before I bowled. My action in 1971 was roughly similar to the sling-shot style of Jeff Thomson, except that I was more chest-on than Thomson. There the similarity ends as I was never as fast or as devastating.

Quite rightly, I wasn't selected for the first two games of the tour as I tried to sort out my bowling. By the time I'd patched it up a little, I was ready to play against Northamptonshire and ready for another shock to the system. It was the first time I'd bowled at county batsmen and I was shattered to see how comfortably they coped with my big inswingers that had proved too good for many reckless Pakistani batsmen. The English simply played forward with bat and pad close together and smothered the swing; and the wickets were so slow that I couldn't bowl bouncers at them. My two weapons in my fast bowling armoury were negated, yet I refused to accept my limitations and kept plugging away.

I remember Gordon Greenidge hitting me for a massive six that disappeared over a distant chimney yet I got three wickets in that innings against Hampshire, including the great Barry Richards — although he got himself out to me, rather than through my efforts. Luckily for my analysis, I retired from the match with a strained thigh muscle. By this time my only chance of getting wickets was by element of surprise: the batsmen didn't know where the ball would go and sometimes they'd be astonished to find one pitching on a good length. One day an umpire summed up my bowling beautifully. As I took off my sweater to start a new spell, he shouted down to wicket to the batsman: 'Right arm over, anywhere' which I found amusing. I saw myself as a batsman, even though I was put in at number ten most of the time; the respectable thirties I picked up here and there reinforced my confidence in my batting. As far as I was concerned, bowling was just a passport to get into the Test side and once selected, my double hundred in my first Test would mean that bowling was no longer necessary.

Normally, a tour party would never have to consider the Imran Khan of 1971 for a Test place. Unfortunately for Pakistan, this was not so. Saleem Altaf and Sarfraz Nawaz were ruled out of the first Test through injuries, so the selectors just had to turn to me. I realised that bowling at men like Cowdrey and Edrich wouldn't be easy, but I was certain I had been included for my batting potential. Therefore, on the night before the Edgbaston Test, it seemed perfectly natural that I should lie awake, conjuring up the dramatic scene where Majid and I would steer Pakistan to a brilliant victory with a dashing partnership.

On the first morning of the Test, I unwittingly revealed another example of my incredible cricketing naïvety. Casually I mentioned to Majid that I was still having some trouble with my run-up. He offered to help me and took me out to the nets. Majid told me to go and organise my run-up and watched as I strode out, turned and marked the start of my run. Majid looked puzzled and said 'Didn't you count your steps when you walked back?' I told him that all I ever did was walk back a few yards, then look back to the stumps and stop there if it felt long enough. Majid gave me a very strange look which I didn't understand then but do now. He simply muttered something like 'Just play the match and we will sort it out afterwards.' I was due to play in my first Test and bowl at great batsmen — yet I didn't have a proper run-up! My run-up would vary by yards and I could start off on either foot depending on how it felt at the time.

I had much to think about over the next few days as our batsmen played superbly to get over 600. Zaheer played a truly memorable knock of 274 — an impressive response to those who said he wouldn't get a run in English conditions with such a high backlift. I shall never forget my first over in Test cricket. It was bowled to Colin Cowdrey, a man who was playing first-class cricket before I was even born. Astonishingly, I almost bowled him in that initial over — but that was only because he sliced an inswinging full toss perilously close to his leg stump. The first four deliveries were all full tosses and Cowdrey was so startled that he failed to score off any of them. It was just my ill fortune that the ball was swinging around like a boomerang in the cloudy atmosphere and I hadn't a clue how to control the swing. At the other end, Asif Masood was bowling beautifully, while I kept everyone on edge, wondering where the next delivery would land. At the end of each over, I stole a sheepish look at Intikhab, my captain; finally he came up to me and explained that an inswinger should start outside the off-stump, not outside leg. Perhaps he thought I was bowling erratically on purpose. After our little chat, the first ball of my next over landed straight into the hands of a bewildered Asif Masood — at leg slip! Soon I was put out of my misery and taken off. The rest of my bowling spells in that Test were brief and I didn't take a wicket, although I bowled more tidily than in those first five dreadful overs. England avoided defeat, thanks to rain and a lack of adequate seam bowling support for Asif Masood. With Sarfraz or Saleem to back him up, we would surely have won.

Although that first Test was a nightmare for me, it was a vastly encouraging one for the rest of the team. The myths of English superiority were shattered at Edgbaston and we would have won at Leeds if our batting hadn't buckled under the pressure and we lost by just 25 runs. Later that summer, India exposed England's fallibility and if our side had been more experienced in Test cricket, we would have played more professionally and won the series. One remark from Zaheer at Edgbaston underlined our inferiority complex in that first Test. He returned to our dressing-room after scoring a wonderful 274 only to ask Majid if he really thought he'd played well! This after scoring 274 against bowlers of the calibre of Ward, Lever, Illingworth and Underwood in his first Test innings in England at the age of twenty-four! We teased Zaheer about that remark for years afterwards, but it showed how much he and the side needed constant reassurance. All that changed after Edgbaston.

While the reputation of our side rose, that of Imran Khan sank without trace. I am convinced that if the tour had ended after the Edgbaston Test, I would have given up serious cricket. It had suddenly dawned on me that I was a bad player; no longer could I delude myself about my batting ability, because a top score of 36 not out did nothing to indicate latent talent. I was treated like a novice who wasn't good enough by the rest of the players and I knew that no matter how well I fared in the remainder of the tour, I would never play in another Test. The facts were brutally spelt out to me one day by Sadiq Mohammed. We were playing one of the counties and Sadiq was told to field in the bat/pad position at short leg. Sadiq, mindful of the dangers of such a position, pointed to me and said to the captain: 'Put him there instead — he's not going to be playing any more Tests on this trip.'

The turning point came at Selkirk, Scotland. Asif Iqbal and Aftab Gul sat talking about me, aware that I could hear them. Their verdict was that I would be lucky to get into the second eleven of an English club side, let alone a county team. They made no attempt to hide their scorn of my abilities: the remarks were made to hurt me. I was so angry and humiliated that I vowed to prove them wrong; I would go back to the drawing-board and sort out my bowling action. I'd make myself indispensable to the side as an all-rounder even if it meant working myself into the ground. I decided that I wouldn't make myself available for Test cricket again until I was sure I'd no longer be humiliated by my own inabilities and my team-mates' scorn. Some of the team were talking behind my back about how lucky I was to get on the tour — the slur of nepotism was bandied about. In retrospect, I can see their point but at the time I was deeply hurt. I deserved to be taken down a peg or two because I was so arrogant at the start of the tour but soon I became isolated. I was just over eighteen and had never been away from home before; Majid had gone back to Cambridge and I was short of friends. The younger members of the party were treated like schoolboys, which I suppose is what we were. We had to be in bed by a certain time, no matter what stage of the game; once Talat Ali, Azmat Rana and I stuffed pillows into our beds in the hotel and slipped out to a disco. We were impressionable youngsters dazzled by the bright lights. Unfortunately we were caught and fined £2 each. During the M.C.C. dinner at Lord's our manager made a funny speech. Every member of the tour party was placed on a different table to get acquainted with our hosts and the usual crop of cricket fans: there we sat, squirming with embarrassment as our manager told the assembly that English cricket had taught us how to behave properly. He got completely carried away, informing the M.C.C. members that we owed it to the M.C.C. and cricket for teaching us how to hold a knife and fork properly! All of our party looked down in total embarrassment except Azmat Rana, one of our batsmen: he sat there, grinning from ear to ear during the tirade, blissfully unaware of the gist of the manager's remarks. He was the only one in the tour party who couldn't understand a word of English!

For me that was one of the rare moments of humour on that tour. I don't blame Intikhab, my captain; he had enough to do and keeping morale high was more important than worrying too much about a young player who had started the tour convinced he knew everything about the game. I deserved my misery. There was just too big a gap between first-class cricket in Pakistan and International cricket. The best players in our squad were also experienced in English cricket. Luckily I was about to take steps in getting some of that precious experience. Worcestershire had approached me in Pakistan earlier that year after I'd scored fifty against them batting at number ten. We had reached a verbal agreement just before my disastrous Test debut. If they developed cold feet after Edgbaston, they didn't tell me! I said I wanted to complete my studies with a view to getting into Oxford or Cambridge and they got me admission as a border at the Worcester Royal Grammar School. I played some second eleven cricket after the Pakistan tour ended, with little success. I wasn't surprised at that as I realised my game needed a radical overhaul and a strong dose of realism on my part. I knew county cricket would give me the necessary experience if I worked hard. The home truths of Selkirk earlier that summer made me obsessed with being good enough. I would never make myself available for selection until I felt I was good enough to be in the team. I realise now that if I had gone back to Pakistan after the UK tour, I would just have studied, gone into the Civil Service and left Test cricket for good. Many players in Pakistan like me have been destroyed after just one Test. English county cricket was to help me in my cricket rehabilitation.

3   Searching for Self-Respect

My first winter in England was educational in more ways than one. I had not forgotten my promise to my parents that my studies wouldn't be neglected once the 1971 tour was over, while my failure on the cricket field gnawed away at me. My immediate goals were a place at Oxford or Cambridge and cricketing respectability.

The first few months at Worcester Grammar School were the most difficult; getting back to my studies took all my will power and concentration. Thanks to excellent teaching standards and the cold I succeeded. It was such an odd feeling for me to spend days without seeing the sun, yet the cold forced me to stay indoors and study while keeping warm. I had to do a two-year 'A' Level course in nine months without proper notes and although I found the sheer discipline of studying rather difficult after a long lay-off, I was nevertheless pleased with my progress. I suppose my fellow-boarders were slightly in awe of a boy who had already played Test cricket, but deep down I knew there was little for me to brag about. It wasn't until after three months of joining Worcester Grammar that the urge to improve my cricket started to come back. The school gymnasium housed my evening cricket matches with a tennis ball, as I strove to improve my bowling action. I had watched the great Australian Graham McKenzie during the 1971 season and I tried to model myself on him: that was fine as long as I bowled slowly, but as soon as I tried for some extra pace, I ended up with my usual wayward action.

Try as I might, I couldn't get out of my slinging bowling action. I was near to despair when a chance encounter in the street gave me new hope. John Parker had joined the Worcestershire staff at the same time as me; a New Zealander, he was a limited batsman who nevertheless played with distinction for his country. More relevant for me, he was a walking, talking M.C.C. coaching book who knew a great deal about technique. When I told him about my problems, he suggested I should take a jump just before I delivered the ball — this would turn my body round and get my footwork right. I already knew the importance of getting side-on, so that I could be in a position to bowl the outswinger, rather than my predictable inswingers. During my sessions in the school gymnasium, I tried to incorporate my run-up with the bowling action, rather than as separate entities. One evening, John Parker came down to view my new action. He looked worried and he told me to think very carefully about changing my style, otherwise I might lose what little natural assets I had. In fact he told me that I should go back to my original action but I had decided that I would stick to my new method, incorporating the jump. I was in a great dilemma: I desperately wanted to improve on the existing model, which wasn't good enough. I thought my original action had no potential for improvement and a radical overhaul was necessary. For the rest of that winter I practised hard with a tennis ball, searching for rhythm, turning my step into a jump.

By April, and the start of a new season, the action felt satisfactory to me. Schools cricket proved the ideal vehicle for experiment; the standard was poor and I simply bowled up to twenty overs on the trot at one end. This helped stabilise my action; I now had a measured run-up, and with a body movement that was a little more side-on, I could bowl the ball that went away from the bat on occasions. The haul of wickets I picked up also did my confidence the world of good. Unfortunately, that was soon shattered when I played Second Eleven cricket for Worcestershire. The senior players on the staff thought I could bat reasonably, but they were unimpressed by my bowling. Glenn Turner was rather cynical and told me: 'Get it into your head — you're never going to be quick enough to be physically dangerous to batsmen'. Basil D'Oliveira and Norman Gifford, two very experienced and likeable players, were more considerate and encouraging, but they didn't disagree with Turner, advising me to concentrate on my batting and just swing bowling.

I kicked my heels in the second team during that 1972 season at New Road and I found the cricket terribly tedious. The games were farcical, with everything dependent upon declarations; first team players who were out of form just treated them as practice matches. There seemed little concerted effort to achieve positive results, a situation that is anathema to my competitive nature. A far cry indeed from the cut and thrust of the matches at Zaman Park! As a result, my performances were fairly ordinary for the second eleven. Things weren't exactly ideal between me and the management at Worcester. The two men who had fixed me up there, Joe Lister, the Secretary, and Wing Commander Shakespeare, the President, were no longer at New Road when I reported for cricket in 1972 and I found a few things entirely different from the terms we had discussed. For a start, my wages had been reduced and secondly, John Parker was to be specially registered ahead of me. There was room for only one more overseas player and they decided it was to be John. Unless I got into Oxford at the end of the season I would be sacked — residence at Oxford would entitle me to be deemed an English player for registration purposes. I felt very upset by all this and never felt any loyalty for them: everything had been verbally agreed, and I had been promised regular county cricket, but the new regime wouldn't have any of it. I faced the prospect of going back to Pakistan if I failed to get into Oxford and cricket would have to take a back seat until I graduated. Therefore my ambitions of regaining my place in the Pakistan team were a pipe dream unless I got into Oxford; I had realised that I could only improve satisfactorily as a cricketer if I had regular involvement in English first-class cricket. I was confused and hurt that Worcestershire didn't think enough of me during that 1972 season. By the end of it I was only marginally a better cricketer — my new action was an improvement in my eyes, though not to anyone else and I could now actually bowl outswingers on occasions. I was slower but more accurate and all the experienced players at New Road had dismissed my chances of ever bowling fast. Their verdict was chastening to me because my ambitions to bowl fast had been fuelled by the sight that summer of two of the greatest of their kind — John Snow and Dennis Lillee. During the England–Australia series, my eyes were glued to Snow and Lillee. About that time it became an ambition of mine to bowl fast. This was the first time I had watched genuine fast bowling of such high calibre and I found it very exciting.

Well, luck was at hand at last. My 'A' level grades were good enough to get me into Oxford. My cricket and academic education was to run on parallel lines for another three years. I entered Keble College in October 1972 to read geography, switching to politics and economics in my second year. My priorities were sorted out very quickly — hard academic work in the winter, leaving plenty of time for cricket in the summer term. I loved Oxford — there was so much fun, so much to do and see. It was a breath of fresh air after the claustrophobia of school and the one track life of a county cricketer. The cricket was equally refreshing and helped to make me a far better player. We tried our very best to win and worked hard at quashing the inferiority complex many feel when they come up against the county sides. This atmosphere got the best out of me, because the team looked to me for inspiration with both bat and ball, just because I was a Test player. It was best of all in my first year: it was a good team, we were all good friends and I was encouraged to bowl fast. I began to believe in myself and the feeling was rather special after the torment of the previous year. Regular competition against experienced first-class cricketers is a great help to Oxford and Cambridge players, even if the gulf in ability is vast. I batted number four and opened the bowling in my three years at Oxford and my game improved enormously in the face of such pressure.

In my first season with Oxford, I picked up a few fifties with the bat without coming to terms completely with responsibility. My bowling was, for the most part, only medium-pace; partly because I had to do a lot of bowling. Indeed I used to complain bitterly if my captain tried to take me off! Now and then, I'd slip myself and let a few fast deliveries go — despite being a medium pacer, I had the temperament of a fast bowler and hated being hit to the boundary — and when it all clicked together for a couple of overs, the effect was exhilerating. My team-mates always egged me on to bowl fast, and although I often ended up spraying the ball all over the place, I felt sufficiently encouraged by my progress by the time term ended.

The feeling of confidence soon ebbed away when I got back to Worcester for the final part of the 1973 season. After failing at number four in the first couple of matches, I was demoted to seven in the batting order. My bowling still didn't impress the seniors; they kept drumming 'line and length' into my head, and I was made to bowl inswing to a packed legside field with the wicket-keeper standing by. Fairly effective in the limited over matches, I suppose, but not my idea of cricket. I hated being a negative bowler, relying on a batsman's mistake for a dismissal. I wanted to quicken up my bowling but everyone kept saying I was a batsman who could bowl a bit. Yet every time I batted I was far too tense and failed miserably. So at the end of the 1973 season, my reputation was almost as low as that of 1971 — I was seen as an erratic, fast-scoring batsman who could bowl defensively in one-day cricket.

I managed to break away from that generalisation in the following season. I was elected the 1974 Oxford captain and my performances with both bat and ball picked up dramatically. Responsibility made me a better player: the team was almost entirely comprised of freshmen who were easily overawed against household names they hero-worshipped. I started getting big hundreds — 170 against Northants and 160 against the Indian tourists — as I played with more discretion than ever before. At last I managed to bowl fast for consistent periods. The Oxford players, particularly my good friend Guy Waller, kept urging me to bowl quicker and after the brainwashing I'd experienced at Worcester, I had my misgivings. I felt that I gave away too many runs by tearing in like Lillee, and using too many slips and gullies but other considerations swayed me — I got bored bowling tightly at county batsmen who came just to polish up their averages and we needed a strike bowler to retaliate after our batsmen had been given the bouncer treatment. I also knew I had the temperament for fast bowling, rather than cunning 'line and length' stuff, so I kept attacking. One of my best bowling performances at the Parks was getting Geoff Boycott out for 89 with a beautiful inswinger during a very good spell against Yorkshire. I had been fired up by his rather patronising attitude to me before the match, when he'd suggested it wasn't worth going out to the middle to toss the coin. On that day, everything clicked and I was delighted with the delivery that got Boycott.

My form with Oxford was sufficiently impressive to earn a recall to the Pakistan squad for the tour to England in the latter part of the 1974 season. The news was sweet indeed to me: I felt I was at last making strides as a cricketer worthy of playing for my country. That soon proved debatable early in the tour when we played Warwickshire; their opening batsman John Jameson took such a liking to my bowling that he hammered me for sixty runs in just four overs! Not only was I embarrassed but my colleagues were furious with me because a curfew was imposed on us that evening. In those days there was a misguided tradition among the Pakistan management that whenever we performed badly on the field, it was due to a hectic social life, so we were treated like naughty schoolboys and confined early to our rooms. As a result, Jameson's assault on me brought some dirty looks in my direction.

Occasional curfews apart, that was the most successful tour of England yet taken by Pakistan. We finished the trip unbeaten and I am sure that one of the reasons was that we had toughened up in recent years and were more used to the pressures and tensions of Test cricket. Eighteen months earlier, we had lost 3–0 in Australia and Ian Chappell's forceful captaincy had made an impression on our players. Sarfraz, in particular, came back from Australia a far better bowler. I even noticed the change in our captain, Intikhab, one of the gentler characters in the team. It was quite a contrast to the easy-going ways of the English county sides, who are generally fairly passive in their relations with the opposition. They see each other so often over the seasons that they become good friends and somehow they lack the spark on the field to give of their best against men whom they like. The Pakistan side of 1974 was much more competitive than English county teams, and our confidence bordered on arrogance at times. I found myself being swept along on this tide of aggression.

Despite my extra pace and improved control, I might have blossomed into a top-order batsman if the events of 1974 had gone a little differently. If I'd batted at number four in that Pakistan side, I am sure that I would never have looked back and that my bowling would have decreased in its influence. I felt that I was improving rapidly with the bat, yet our line-up was so strong that I never really got the chance to prove it. Sometimes I came in as low as number eight on that tour and the only time I really had a chance to shine was in the Leeds Test — I scored 23 and 31 in a low-scoring match and felt I played well in two crises. I'm afraid that my attitude to batting has never been very balanced when I am placed low down in the order. I feel that it's almost impossible to make much of an impact below number six in the list, especially in as powerful a batting side as Pakistan's. Time after time, I have come in at seven or eight when a declaration is imminent and a slog is needed to top off a huge score. Often I have walked in to bat in a Test with hardly any match practice behind me and I have to spend the first few overs groping for some semblance of form — the penalty for having prolific batsmen in the team, I suppose.

In 1974, Zaheer added another double hundred to his Test tally — 240 at the Oval on the kind of slow, flat wicket he loves — but the best knock in that innings came from Majid. He scored a beautiful 98 in his typically effortless style, then, equally typically, he was bowled playing a sleepy shot at Underwood. At this time Majid was at his peak and one of the best batsmen in the world. He played the quick bowlers better than any of our batsmen, a fact he proved to a wider audience in the following year when in the World Cup, he was hooking Lillee, Thomson and Roberts in front of square. The best innings I saw from Majid came on that 1974 tour, in a one-day international against England. We needed 245 in 50 overs on a seamers' wicket in cloudy weather against bowlers of the calibre of Bob Willis, Peter Lever, Chris Old and Derek Underwood. Majid made 109 and we won with more than seven overs to spare. It was a remarkable effort, all the more astonishing because he usually liked a fast wicket to play his wristy shots. Although some thought he was a better player in the middle order, I always felt he was an ideal opener; there was less pressure on him at the start, he could relax and play his shots through an attacking field before a bowler could get his line and length. Although he was a relaxed and calm person, Majid thought deeply about the game and he was a man of honour. He was so appalled at the back-stabbing in the Glamorgan team that he had no hestitation in leaving English cricket once he thought the team wasn't supporting him. The Glamorgan players seemed to blame all their failures on Majid without realising that their rare victories normally stemmed from his brilliance — yet when they were lying at the bottom of the table in 1976, Majid was the scapegoat. He heard the whispering campaign and resigned, even though he was due a benefit in the following season. I wonder how many players would have the courage to walk out on their chance of a benefit?

Majid's decline as a batsman dates from the time when he left English cricket. He needed regular exposure to top-class bowlers and he didn't get that in Pakistan domestic competition. Yet between 1972 and 1977, he was truly magnificent and best in our team. His advice on fast bowling was invaluable to me on that 1974 tour. He told me I had a perfectly good action and to take no notice of the Worcester attitude of just bowling line and length. His advice was to put more emphasis on pace and to remember that Test batsmen don't get out to accurate medium-pacers all that often especially outside England. I also knew that Pakistan lacked a genuine pace bowler and that just possibly I could fill that gap.

The following year I was still raw and wayward in my bowling. When I occasionally took the advice of the older players at Worcester, I bowled accurately and managed to swing the ball — yet I was extremely sharp sometimes, even though I wasn't tight enough and lost some of my swing. Gifford and D'Oliveira were happy enough with the improvement in my bowling, but were much more enthusiastic about my batting, predicting great things for me once I curbed my rashness. The fact that I averaged just ten for Worcestershire in first-class cricket didn't deter Gifford and D'Oliveira and I must say I was very grateful for their support.

The problem of being an all-rounder wasn't the only thing to occupy my mind during that summer of 1975. I sat my finals at Oxford and went through agonies during the World Cup. It was the first time such a competition had been staged for cricket and I really felt Pakistan had a great chance. I'm afraid my passionate support for my country on the cricket field had a direct bearing on my exam performances. To my surprise, I was called up for the match against Australia, which was slap in the middle of my finals. After finishing two of my papers on the Friday, I took a train to Leeds and arrived at the team's hotel at four o'clock, the morning of the match. We lost the game through bad batting; it was there for the taking, after a brilliant innings by Majid but once he was out, we were unable to withstand the relentless pressure of Dennis Lillee. I took my disappointment back to Oxford and arrived at three in the morning, grimly contemplating the rest of my finals. I was exhausted and, predictably, went down with 'flu. By this time I was in no fit state for my last two papers on the following Wednesday and the fact that Pakistan was playing West Indies at Edgbaston made matters even worse. It was the kind of match that happens once in a lifetime, their last pair, Murray and Roberts, needed 64 to win in 14 overs, and somehow they got them with two balls to spare. I must have been the only student at Oxford who wasn't celebrating the end of the finals, knowing we were out of the World Cup.

Although sadness accompanied the end of my time at Oxford, I shall always look back with fondness to those three years. I had no regrets about taking that time out of my Test career to study, even though I might have been in the Test arena. My cricket continued to improve at Oxford and the mental challenges involved in studying helped me in my attitude to cricket. I became more logical and analytical about my game and the discipline of scholastic work undoubtedly stood me in good stead later on when I needed to sit down and sort out where my cricket career was going.

When I rejoined the Pakistan squad for the final, meaningless game against Sri Lanka, they were still in a state of shock after Edgbaston. No one could believe it: for years afterwards, the survivors from that amazing match used to talk about the way it just slipped out of our fingers. The pros and cons were debated endlessly but one fundamental point was always accepted — we could have won the World Cup in 1975 if we'd kept our nerve. Little did I know it, but we would be saying the same thing after the World Cup of 1979.

At the end of that 1975 season, I went home to Pakistan for the first time in four years. A crop of talented young batsmen were coming through — men like Javed Miandad, Musassar Nazar and Mohsin Khan — but we were still desperately short of opening bowlers. The cricket was very competitive, partly because our national side had been faring well in recent years and also because all the top players were playing in Pakistan, in the absence of a Test series that winter. Initially I was written off by most journalists, because it took me fully three months to acclimatise to the heat and the totally different wickets. Eventually I bowled fast and straight on the hard wickets and managed to swing the ball enough to claim 33 batsmen in the four pentangular matches. I realised that I would get nowhere on the hard, slow wickets by bowling English-style medium pace to a defensive field; the only way I was going to get men out was through speed. That trip to Pakistan made up my mind — from then on, I would be a fast bowler or nothing at all. The days of compromise were over. I would continue to work at my action, to modify it in certain areas, but it would all be geared towards blasting batsmen out.

I returned to England a much better all-round player. I had developed a fondness for the hook shot in Pakistan, because so many bouncers were bowled at me in retaliation for my efforts. For a time I got obsessed with playing the hook shot and it brought me many runs (and a few dismissals), but I had learned to stay longer at the wicket, learning more and more about batting. Worcestershire put me in at number four and I never looked back after getting a hundred in my first match. I averaged forty in the championship (with four centuries) and over fifty in the John Player League. I was also top of the bowling averages and at last Basil D'Oliveira and Norman Gifford had stopped nagging me about keeping things tight — every now and then I managed to bowl a genuinely fast spell and I could tell they were impressed! The hot, dry summer meant I could bowl on some fiery wickets and I sent down many bouncers that season. I realised that I would get my fair share of them as a batsman, so I made sure they were returned with interest. I must admit I did overdo the bouncer in those days, I would regularly bowl four in my first over of a new ball spell just to let the batsman know I was quicker than before. I wouldn't have been able to do that a year earlier: I was so much more confident now after my good season in Pakistan, and I knew that if I failed with the ball, there was always my batting as compensation. The county match against Lancashire had underlined my emerging qualities and I scored 111 not out and took thirteen wickets.

One of the reasons I was changing from a medium pacer to a fast bowler was my temperament. I have always hated taking a beating lying down — something essential for a medium pacer. Consequently I would find myself on various occasions being hit, forgetting about swing, line and length and just seeing blood in front of my eyes. It was during such moments of anger that an increase of adrenalin would add an extra yard or two to my pace. Somehow my action began to change to accomodate this extra pace.

At last I was worth my place in a county side as a batsman and a bowler. It had taken a long time to convince the sceptics that I possessed genuine cricketing ability. I must admit it took almost as long for me to be sure of it. Yet I knew I still had much to learn. My bowling action was not yet properly co-ordinated and my batting needed a cool head at times. Before that could happen, I needed to sort out my future in English cricket. Little did I realise what was in store for me. But at least at the end of the 1976 season for the first time I felt confidence in my ability as an all-rounder. I knew I had improved as a cricketer.

4 A Year of Rows

Within a few months of the end of the 1976 season, I had become embroiled in three disputes which didn't help my image. My detractors would sum up the three disputes thus — I had walked out on my English county, then I had held the Pakistan selectors to ransom for more money and finally I had turned my back on my country to sign for Kerry Packer. My side of the story on all three controversies hasn't really been fully aired until now.

First my dispute with Worcestershire. Quite simply I no longer wanted to play for the county because I couldn't face the prospect of spending six months of my life in Worcester. I liked the players and I owed a lot to people like Gifford and D'Oliveira but there was no chance of a compromise when I told the committee at the end of the 1976 season that I was finished at New Road. They were shocked, because they had no idea I was unhappy, and indignant because they were worried about the members' reaction — especially after weathering a storm a year earlier when some of the county's best players had been summarily sacked. It was made quite clear to me that I owed loyalty to the county — despite the misunderstanding about my engagement in 1972 I tried to explain my reasons, but kept coming up against a blank wall of incomprehension. I simply found Worcester a boring place: I was not a machine who could be switched on and off at the start of a day's play, I needed some life away from the cricket, especially as I never enjoyed the pub scene which was all the town offered. I missed Oxford; I'd made good friends there and playing cricket with guys of the same age and outlook had been so stimulating. Much as I liked Worcestershire's players, I felt isolated an hour after play ended, they would all drift off with their families and go home for the evening or to other pubs. I didn't expect any special favours from them, it was more a case that I didn't fit in with the pace of life at Worcester. All of my friends from Grammar School days had left the area, and I found myself driving down to London whenever I had a free day. I even joined the local library and got through about four books a week! Although totally involved in the cricket during the day, I found myself quite redundant in the evenings. I used to long for the away trips, to see something different. Since pleasure was the main reason for playing county cricket — it certainly wasn't the money — I decided that I needn't subject myself to this kind of life.

I had various meetings with the Secretary, Mike Vockins, and the committee before I left for Pakistan in September, 1976. They were convinced I had been poached by another county and offered a big sum of money to leave New Road; in vain did I plead that money had nothing at all to do with it. Some of the remarks were rather unsavoury: one committee member said in front of me, 'The reason why he's going is because there aren't enough women in this town to satisfy him.' They tried the carrot and the stick treatment — the carrot in the shape of better financial terms, and the stick with the warning that any proposed move of mine to another county would be opposed by Worcestershire. I was told that they had evidence that I'd been negotiating with other counties while still under contract and that I'd be banned from championship cricket. Yet my mind was made up. It was a question of values; I wouldn't subject myself to another six months of life in Worcester. If necessary, I would finish with county cricket.

The slurs about disloyalty hurt me. When I joined Worcestershire in 1971, my loyalty was to the two men who had asked me there — Joe Lister and Wing Commander Shakespeare. Yet when I reported to New Road in 1972, they had gone and the new administration soon let me know that things weren't going to turn out as I'd expected. My salary of £35 a week was reduced to £25 and I was placed behind John Parker in the queue for special registration. Entry into Oxford saved my county career prospects, not any effort on the part of Worcestershire. In the summer of 1976 I felt I had been let down by Worcestershire over my accommodation. They had known for six months that I would need somewhere to stay in Worcester on my return from the Pakistan domestic season and I understood that everything was in hand. I had to sleep on Glen Turner's floor for the first five days, then the club put me up in what I thought was the lousiest hotel I've ever seen — the door used to be locked at eleven at night! After six weeks, I managed to find a flat of my own and then the club made me pay half the hotel bill. This after saying they'd have my accommodation ready for me when I returned in April. How could I have organised it from Pakistan? I felt my performances in the 1976 season were more than enough to repay whatever loyalty I might have owed to Worcestershire — only Gifford bowled more overs, just two other batsmen surpassed my runs tally and I took most wickets and topped the bowling averages. Yet I know I was paid less than John Inchmore, the medium-pace bowler who had not yet made much of an impact on county cricket. This is not meant to belittle John Inchmore, more to point out that my all-round value to the team was surely greater, yet I was getting less money. I felt I was being exploited, while the club was peddling emotive stuff to the press on the lines of: 'We paid for his education and now he walks out on us because he doesn't like sitting on his own, watching television.' It was totally untrue about the club paying for my education — that was taken care of by my parents.

Throughout the winter of 1976–77, the club was in contact with me, trying to change my mind. At one stage, Mike Vockins suggested I live in London and drive up to the games at Worcester! I could just picture struggling out of my car after a trip up the motorway. The threats continued, but I couldn't believe the English legal system would allow Worcestershire to get away with banning me from county cricket for life. On 1 January 1977, I was at last able to negotiate with other counties and I agreed to join Sussex. I liked the idea of trying my hardest for a dynamic captain like Tony Greig and looked forward to playing with an enthusiastic young team at Hove, on an ideal cricket wicket that favours the stroke-maker and the bowler who can put some effort into his work. London would only be about fifty miles away. The prospect of a new career with Sussex was an enticing one.

I hadn't bargained for the obstinacy of Worcestershire. They opposed my move to Sussex and the result was a hearing at Lord's. I found the experience very strange. I was put in a witness box and cross-examined at great length about my motives for leaving Worcester. I met the same kind of incomprehension when I stated that I just could not live there anymore; when asked why I hadn't said this in previous years, I pointed out that 1976 was my first full season there. The whole atmosphere was as if I'd committed a heinous crime. I felt a strong sense of injustice because Worcestershire failed to admit any responsibility for the breakdown between us. I knew for a fact that several other players had moved counties at the same time by putting their clubs into a corner, demanding a ludicrous pay increase and then asking for release when negotiations had broken down. There was no fuss about those kind of dealings, yet here I was, pilloried for being totally honest about the situation. Ted Dexter confirmed this to me — he said I should have walked into the office and demanded the earth, thereby contriving a gulf that could never be bridged. I didn't think that was necessary, I felt that acting sincerely would be the proper course. I should have known better; my experiences stemming from a verbal agreement in 1971 with Worcestershire had not been very pleasant.

The committee at Lord's initially supported Worcestershire and I was banned for the whole of the 1977 season. I was shattered; some of my Pakistani friends told me such a thing couldn't be possible and luckily, Sussex agreed. They hired a brilliant lawyer, called Quinton Barry, who argued my case with impressive conviction. As a result, I served a period of suspension and managed to play for Sussex in the final month of the 1977 season. The decision by Lord's stirred up quite a furore amoung county cricketers and there was talk of some players refusing to play against me, while their union, the Cricketers' Association officially deplored my transfer without listening to my version of the events. Slurs were bandied about concerning disloyalty by overseas players, but I considered that merely a stick with which they could beat world-class cricketers who had done a great deal to keep some counties solvent and raise the standard of county cricket. It was considered reasonable for England players like Bob Willis to leave Surrey and join Warwickshire because he wasn't getting regular cricket. Three years later, Barry Wood left Lancashire for Derbyshire after picking up a huge tax-free benefit. All he served was a month's suspension. It was easy to paint the cliche picture — Imran Khan, the prima donna Pakistani who'll only play cricket for a team near the bright lights — and even more convenient to forget that loyalty should be a two-way thing.

While locked in my bitter wrangling with Worcestershire during the 1976–77 winter, I also faced a ban from Test cricket, and indeed all cricket in Pakistan. That was the threat from the Board of Cricket Control. The trouble blew up on the eve of our three-Test series at home to New Zealand. For some time our senior players had been complaining about the low rates of pay awarded for representing our country in Tests. We received 1,000 rupees per Test (about £50), while across the border (in a country with a better exchange rate and lower cost of living), the Indian players received 7,000 rupees (about £350). At this stage, we were the lowest paid Test cricketers in the world, even worse than the unfashionable New Zealanders, and yet our international standing was very high, especially after our 1974 tour of England.

Just before the first Test, our senior players urged our captain, Mushtaq Mohammed, to take our grievances to the head of the board, A.H. Kardar, a former Test captain with a reputation for autocratic treatment of players. Kardar refused to even discuss a possible revision of fees for Tests and tours and just to show who was really the boss, he authorised changes in our side for the first Test. On the first morning of the game, Intikhab and Wasim Raja turned up at the Gaddafi Stadium in their whites. Neither had been named in the twelve for the Test. Mushtaq was called into the Board's office and told that they were to play instead of Farrukh Zaman and Sikander Bakht, who were due to make their debuts. They were busy loosening up after sleepless nights, trying to calm their nerves when the news was broken to them. Mushtaq had two alternatives — to resign or accept the dictatorial instructions. He gave in.

On the night before the second Test, the entire squad met to discuss Kardar's policy. We agreed to draft a letter to the Board, stating that unless we had a guarantee that our request for more money should at least be considered, we would have no option but to pull out of the forthcoming Test. No one dissented and our letter was sent to the Board the day before the match was due to start. It had little effect on Kardar — at eight o'clock we received a telegram from the Board warning us that

The two-month old Imran with his mother and at one and a half years.

cricket at home in the garden.

The Aichison College ... et Team 1964. Imran is second from the left in the front row.

The Aitchison College Cricket Team 1968 with Imran third from the right
in the front row.

1971 and the Pakistan team is presented to the Queen.

On the attack, 1974; in the background is England captain Mike Denness.

Benson and Hedges Final 1976. Imran bowling for Worcestershire and *below* taking a breather in the outfield.

The final Test, Sydney 1977. Imran bowled for four hours and even tore the shirt sleeve off his bowling arm through striving for extra effort!

Imran is congratulated after taking another wicket in the final Test at Sydney. Altogether he took 12 wickets and received the Man of the Match award.

Amarnath hit by a bouncer in the second Test at Lahore in November 1978. Four years later he came back as the best batsman for India.

Imran at practice before the third Test against England at Karachi 1978. He had flown from Australia where he had been playing for Kerry Packer but, along with Zaheer and Mushtaq did not play.

Jubilation at the fall of an Indian wicket in a tension-charged series against India after a twenty year gap. *Above* after the fall of Prasanna's wicket and

below the fall of Chandrasekhar on the road to an historic win.

anyone who didn't accept the existing terms would be banned from cricket both at home and abroad. That was enough for five of our squad: they couldn't face disrupting their careers and they defected. I was the youngest one left to stand out against the Board. The money was irrelevant to me because I would have paid to play Test cricket if necessary. I was appalled at the highhanded attitude of Kardar and my word had been given. While the remaining seven stood their ground, replacement players were being flown in for the Test. The selectors sat up with us until three in the morning, trying to change our minds but we refused to budge. At seven o'clock, we were woken up by the selectors and told to present ourselves in front of Kardar. At first he saw us individually, hoping no doubt to beat us down with his awesome personality. When that failed, he saw us all together and reiterated the line about our careers being in jeopardy. When he realised we were adamant, he relented. He admitted that our demands were not that unreasonable and that he was unaware that all we desired was a chance to discuss the matter calmly, with give and take on both sides. He agreed to a dialogue at the end of the series in a fortnight. With an hour and a half to go before the start of the second Test — with twenty-four players available for selection — peace had broken out in the Pakistan camp. It only lasted a fortnight.

We were called individually before the Board of Control and presented with our original contracts. If we didn't sign, we would not only miss the forthcoming tour of Australia and the West Indies, but also be banned from Test cricket both at home and abroad. Moreover, we wouldn't get our money for the New Zealand series until a later date. Kardar had told us he would talk about the cash issue at the end of the series, yet here I was, being told to take it or leave it. I had no idea of cricket politics in Pakistan until this time and it was also the first occasion I had experienced distortions in the press. Until then, I had innocently believed everything I read in the papers — surely they wouldn't dare lie? Some journalists with a vested interest in siding with the Board (a promise of a free trip, for example) came up with some remarkable inventions. We were dubbed 'mercenaries' and 'unpatriotic', which conveniently ignored the fact that we were sportsmen playing the game for a living. The press also dredged up the red herring about Karachi and Lahore, trying desperately to see hostility between players from either city; that was never an issue between us at any stage. The Karachi/Lahore matter was only ever important to selection committees, and newspapers.

By now the country was split down the middle. We had two further defections from our ranks. Zaheer felt his position in the team was too insecure following his disastrous series against New Zealand, so he decided to take no chances over the tour to Australia and West Indies, on which he had set his heart. Sarfraz also dropped out — he never got on with Asif Iqbal, one of the other so-called 'rebels'. So there were now six of us — Asif, Mushtaq, Sadiq, Wasim Bari, Majid and myself. For me money was unimportant: I felt the principle of consultation was vital. The Board, in one of its rare statements to us, pointed out that it lacked enough funds, yet it had just sanctioned payments of 20,000 rupees to some illustrious cricketers of the past. In any event, the amount of extra money we wanted was minimal.

We were given a fresh ultimatum to sign the original contracts. When that passed, a new team for the tour of Australia and West Indies was announced, with Intikhab as captain and Zaheer his deputy. The six dissidents were excluded. This sparked off a national uproar, with the press gleefully fanning the flames. Finally, the Government intervened: the Minister of Sports came to hear our side of the story. After much diplomatic shuttling, the Board of Control was overruled and a new committee was set up to pick the tour party. Mushtaq was reinstated as captain; he had already gone back to England, feeling his chances of touring to have disappeared. He also thought that he would actually lose money if he toured on the original terms.

A sequel to our dispute came six months later. The Board of Control announced that in future, a player would receive 5,000 rupees per Test — five times the previous rate. By the time we toured England in 1982, the fee was 13,000 rupees per Test, plus 2,000 rupees for a one-day international. I felt our point had been proved; for too long Pakistan's best cricketers had been treated cheaply.

While the dust settled over the dispute with the Board, I found myself in yet another contentious situation. In April 1977 I signed for Kerry Packer, little realising that the issue would split world cricket for two years. Initially, it was all very clear-cut to me: I was absolutely thrilled by the offer, both on a personal and a professional level. Tony Greig had talked to me while I was in the West Indies and made it clear that I would be one of fourteen players to represent a World XI which would take on an Australian team, containing all their best players. The thirteen other World XI cricketers were out of the top drawer — four South Africans (Pollock, Richards, Procter and Barlow), four West Indians (Roberts, Holding, Richards and Lloyd), three English Test players (Greig, Knott and Underwood) and two from Pakistan (Asif Iqbal and Majid Khan). The fact that I was mentioned in the same breath as that gathering of talent was extremely flattering; just six months before, I had been unsure of my place in the Pakistan side, yet now I had a chance to play with and against the finest cricketers in the world. The money was incredible — 25,000 dollars a year, compared with 100 dollars per Test with Pakistan and the 150 dollars a month I earned from Pakistan International Airways whenever I played in Pakistan.

There was one misgiving for me. England were due to tour Pakistan later that year and I was desperate to play against them. I really wanted to carry on playing Test cricket but Tony Greig smoothed my fears. He pointed out that the cricket administrators would thrash out some sort of compromise with Kerry Packer, because otherwise so many world-class players would be lost to the Test arena. He saw no reason why everyone couldn't sit round a table and come to some sort of arrangement — Packer would get his television rights, his series would be played at a convenient time and his players would still be available for Test cricket. It sounded a sensible line of reasoning to me at the time and I signed the contract. Majid and Asif had little reservation in doing the same and I didn't want to appear reluctant: I was lucky enough in the first place to be asked and I couldn't imagine anyone turning down such a fabulous offer.

The news broke about a month later. All hell broke loose as Greig was denounced as a traitor by the Establishment. The television cameras seemed to spend every day down at Hove, covering each statement from Greig. He was rightly seen as Paker's recruiting agent and the way he calmly and articulately expounded his views only served to infuriate the anti-Packer lobby. Kerry Packer soon realised that his hand would be stronger if he signed more players, so more cricketers were snapped up, including Zaheer and Mushtaq from Pakistan. As the situation polarised, it gradually dawned on me that I was on my way out of Test cricket: Greig's fond hope of a compromise looked very shaky indeed. I hadn't expected things to deteriorate so much, but they did. Back home in Pakistan, the anti-Packer bandwagon rumbled on. Although A.H. Kardar had resigned after the row over our fees, his replacement Mohammad Hussain was a member of the same Board; he announced that the five who had signed for Packer wouldn't be considered for Test cricket because we had failed to ask the Board's permission before entering into the World Series contracts. The papers called us 'avaricious', 'trouble-makers', and 'unpatriotic' and our families had to suffer a campaign of vilification. I couldn't understand why the Pakistan Board sided with Lord's as the dispute didn't affect our country, it was between Packer, the Australian Board and Lord's. The West Indies Board had the right idea, announcing that an independent line would be taken and that they alone would decide who should play for their country. New Zealand and India, on the other hand, were anti-Packer, because neither was affected and they also believed that Lord's was the fount of all cricketing wisdom — the colonial outlook was firmly engrained. I am convinced that the Packer conflict gave our Board an opportunity to get back at the players who had defied them over the Test fees issue a few months earlier. After all, four of the Packer players were also in the group of six who had been involved in the confrontation with the Board.

The attitude of English county cricketers was generally hostile. All sorts of emotions were bandied about at meetings of the Cricketers' Association and the Packer players were pilloried by cricketers who were basically jealous. The bulk of them would never be Test-class, never mind world-class, and they reacted in a small-minded way, ignoring the fact that they would all have signed if asked. The usual sweeping generalisations about overseas players were also tossed about — as for me, a man deep in trouble over his move from Worcester-shire, my defection to Packer was only to be expected.

If the reception in England was that hostile, what could I expect when I returned to Pakistan? After all, I had turned my back on playing for my country because of money, or so it seemd to my detractors. When I arrived at Karachi airport, the attitude of the customs officers was instructive as they eyed my luggage as if I was carrying gold bars. I heard remarks like, 'I'd play for my country for nothing', and it was no use trying to point out that the same applied to me. I had not realised that the situation would escalate in this way. However, some Pakistanis were thrilled that we were to be represented in World Series Cricket and it was often pointed out with glee that Packer had seen fit to ignore all the Indian players. From what I could judge, the public was split down the middle over the Packer Affair — some thought we were traitors, yet many admitted they would have done the same.

Looking back on it now, I still cannot be sure what I would have done if it had been clear that I was to be banned from Tests by signing for Packer. Of course it was the chance of a lifetime and I learned so much from World Series Cricket — yet Test matches are the very pinnacle for me. I lost eighteen months out of my Test career and that saddens me. It was different for the older Pakistan players who signed for Packer because the mystique of Tests had perhaps worn a little thin for some of them. Not for me, I really didn't realise what an uproar Packer would inspire. I don't blame Tony Greig for his persuasive salesmanship, because I believe he was sincere in his optimism for a deal that would satisfy all sides. There was a principle at stake — the amount of money that Test players were receiving under the existing order of things. In Pakistan, we were being paid chicken-feed, while vast crowds thronged the grounds. Where was it all going? Why did the Board take such a dictatorial attitude over a few rupees in 1976 when there was enough money available? The Australians were also bitter about the way the Centenary Test had made fabulous sums of money which had been siphoned off elsewhere. The players had put on a fantastic show at Melbourne, yet the men who cleared up the garbage at the close of play went home with more money! Kerry Packer woke the public to the fact that great entertainers were being paid a pittance: in this sense, cricket followed the lead of tennis, and not before time. Too many administrators failed to see the real importance of Packer and preferred to peddle emotive statements about the greed of some cricketers. They chose to ignore the previous greed of administrations that took little notice of the players who were packing the grounds.

A real sadness to me was that Test cricket was devalued for a year. Too many players represented their countries when their talents were not worthy of such an honour. Missing Tests was agony for me and I was humiliated at the pathetic display of our national side when it toured England in 1978. The Pakistan Board had told the public back home that there were enough quality reserves available to cover for our defection but that proved not to be the case. General Muhammad Zia-Ul Haq, the President of Pakistan, was also Patron-in-Chief of the Board of Control and he acted swiftly after the disastrous tour of England. He instructed the Board to pick the Packer players for the forthcoming series against India. There would have been real trouble if we had lost to India, minus the Packer players. We were being humiliated in Tests because our country had been sucked into a dispute that didn't really concern us. The Board's credibility was at its lowest, some commonsense prevailed. I suppose some people from other countries were amazed that the Government intervened in the matter — surely General Muhammad Zia-Ul Haq had enough on his plate without concerning himself with cricket matters? Well that ignores how important cricket prestige is to Pakistan; it concerns the public and politics is about dealing with the public. Passions run high in Pakistan when we lose badly or triumph spectacularly — either way, the Government of the day is directly concerned with the game and will act accordingly if it thinks necessary.

I learned a lot from the Packer Affair, as I did from the Worcestershire saga and the Kardar row. It seems amazing that all three disputes should have blown up within a space of a few months but they all involved important principles that many critics just didn't understand.

5 Breakthrough in Test Cricket

From October 1976 to April 1977 I was as busy on the cricket field as I was with all the off-field rows. The cricket was considerably more enjoyable than the intrigues; at last I established myself in the Pakistan side. I managed to win at least one Test through my own efforts and at the end of that hectic bout of international cricket, I was being rated as a world-class performer. I took part in eleven Tests during that six month period. It was an exciting time for me and for our side; I advanced rapidly as an opening bowler, while Pakistan lost the tag of a second-rate cricketing nation. With luck, we could have won all three series against New Zealand, Australia and the West Indies. Against New Zealand, I established myself as Sarfraz's opening partner and we bowled many overs between us on typically slow, lifeless pitches. I bowled on average forty overs per Test, but I felt sharp and keen — I'd practised for hours before the series started and I was determined to rebuild my Test career.

There was one major blow to my ambitions of being a Test all-rounder at the start of the series: Mushtaq, my captain, told me I was to bat at number nine. I couldn't believe it; of course we were a very strong batting side, but I had returned from England with a championship average of over forty, while Intikhab — who was to bat at number eight — averaged just eighteen for Surrey. From that point onwards, my batting stagnated until the captaincy made me more responsible in 1982. I was at the peak of my batting prowess, yet I only got four innings in the series — more often with a huge score on the board and the need to slog a few before declaration. If I'd had greater opportunities to bat higher up against the weak New Zealand attack on perfect wickets, I believe my batting would have continued to advance in subsequent years, at the expense of my bowling. I still considered my batting to be superior to my bowling, but I seemed to be the only one with that opinion.

The New Zealand series was a one-sided affair. We piled up massive scores on lifeless tracks and their batting wasn't strong enough to withstand our spinners, plus Sarfraz and myself. To my great pleasure, I dismissed my old mentor, John Parker four times out of six and he was kind enough to remark on the improvement in my bowling — a far cry from the winter evenings in the school gym at Worcester with a tennis ball! It was also pleasant to bowl quickly at Glenn Turner on occasions, I hadn't forgotten his harsh words when I was desperately trying to learn how to be a fast bowler. By now I was quick enough, although I seemed to specialise in in-swingers and bouncers. My run-up was getting better and every now and then it all slipped into place. I now had the desire to dominate batsmen — that killer instinct I'd picked up from Sarfraz — and my body was fit enough to withstand the burden of fast bowling. I learned a lot from bowling on those dead Pakistan wickets, and the experience set me up for the tough assignments in Australia and the West Indies.

As usual, the batsmen grabbed all the headlines in the New Zealand series. I felt the deeds of the bowlers were far more meritorious on such flat wickets, but in Pakistan at that time, the crowds came to see double hundreds, not bouncers. Our batting was awesome on paper, with five of them averaging fifty, but the discovery of the series was Javed Miandad. On his debut he became the youngest to score a century and he proceeded to play a succession of brilliant, quick-footed innings. When I look back at the Javed of 1976 and compare the up-to-date version, I feel slightly frustrated; his gifts are so great, yet he hasn't always done himself justice in the pressure-cooker atmosphere of Test cricket, despite an impressive statistical record. He hasn't really acquitted himself satisfactorily in either Australia or England, despite many dazzling cameo innings. I believe he gets too many fifties without turning them into big hundreds, even though he cashes in on flat wickets in Pakistan. He still has one technical flaw that has been with him since he started in Test cricket — he tends to get off-balance when playing off his legs and gets trapped lbw too often. We have all tried to reason with him about this, but Javed doesn't take constructive criticism terribly well — he functions on instinct. It is so frustrating because he thrives on the big match atmosphere yet he is prone to impetuosity and attacks the bowlers too early. He has one of the best temperaments against the fast men; a real fighter, he has great guts. Javed relishes the challenge yet when he's on top he enters a dangerous phase and loses concentration. He can conjure up shots from all sorts of positions, playing very well off front and back foot, hooking with courage and safety and, a real asset, leaving the ball alone when necessary. His main problem is over-confidence; time after time, I've said to him, 'let the bowlers get you out', but he still goes his own way. Unfortunately he has put on weight since those dazzling days of 1976 (when I thought he was also the best fielder in the world) and I feel he doesn't work as hard at his fitness as he might. I sincerely hope we haven't seen the best of Javed Miandad, because he has so much to offer. He has tended to symbolise the strengths and the defects of our batting in recent years — exotic strokeplay mixed up with suicidal tendencies.

With Javed added to the ranks of our established batsmen, we were very confident as we set off for the

1976–77 tour of Australia and the West Indies. Our treatment at the hands of A.H. Kardar had not affected our relations with the rest of the team, following some initial coolness once we re-assembled after the Government had intervened. The furore was not the best prelude to such as exacting tour, but the sense of expectation among the players was very tangible. Those who'd been to Australia in 1972 were at pains to tell the younger players about the tremendous wickets and the great atmosphere among the crowds. We were up against the best two sides in the world, but saw no reason to feel inferior. They were right: that tour remains for me the highlight of Pakistan cricket. The Australian series was drawn one-all, and although we lost 2–1 to the West Indians, the score could easily have been the other way round. The Pakistan batting was the strongest in the world, even if our willingness to entertain was occasionally marred by inconsistency and inability to withstand pressure.

That 1976 tour to Australia was the most exciting one I've been on. I've never felt my adrenalin flow so much, either before or since. I loved Australia. Most of the wickets were ideal for strokemakers and attacking bowlers and the crowds were vociferous. I enjoy a noisy atmosphere, even if the spectators are biased. I don't mind if they are abusive about my cricket ability as long as they don't get personal. No such problems in Australia — the best place in the world to play cricket, in my opinion.

No Pakistan team in my experience had worked harder before a series until then. Majid initiated a training sequence that really stretched us and we practised and practised in the nets. Our convincing win over New Zealand had sharpened expectations back home and the bitter dispute with Kardar had made us even more determined to do well. The ridiculous tour itinerary even made us more resolute — whoever heard of just one first-class match before the opening Test? No side has ever been so poorly-prepared before a Test series than ours on that trip. We lost to Western Australia; they needed 333 to win in four hours and managed it with ease. As a result of one match, we were written off by the Australian press; Lillee and Thomson had made mincemeat of England and the West Indies in the previous two years, and they would no doubt do the same to us. Our bowling was harshly criticised, even though no one seemed to realise we needed time to adapt to the different conditions. Initially I bowled the wrong line; I was used to bowling at the stumps in England and Pakistan, but that just went straight on and was played away through legside by the Australians who were strong onside players. In such excellent light and with the ball coming onto the bat so quickly, I was murdered. I needed to bowl just outside the off-stump, make the batsmen play at the deliveries and hope that the extra bounce would get them caught in the slips.

The general consensus among the experts was that our seam bowling was not of Test class and certainly the events of the first Test didn't contradict that feeling. I took 1 for 92 in the first innings and bowled just five overs in the second. My seam bowling partners, Sarfraz and Salim Altaf, were also treated harshly and only our spinners looked the part. By then I had realised what I had to do, but it was difficult altering my line after bowling for such a long time in a certain way. I knew I had to adjust, but time wasn't on my side.

Although the seam bowlers were in trouble, the rest of the team played well in that first Test. Australia needed 185 to win with time on their side and for a while they were coasting home. Then Mushtaq produced a magnificent catch to get rid of Greg Chappell and the other batsmen started to look nervous against our spinners. I'd never seen until then a Pakistan side fight with so much grit as on that final day, the fielding and catching were wonderful. In the end, the Australians shut up shop with the game in the balance; they finished 24 runs short with four wickets left. Rodney Marsh and Gary Cosier chickened out of a target of 56 in the last fifteen overs and simply played out time. We were amazed at such a timorous gesture and felt the moral victory was ours. No longer would the Australians be crowing about their alleged invincibility.

The press now staged a somersault in their opinions about us, but the seamers didn't escape from criticism. By the time of the Melbourne Test we were all under pressure. Sarfraz failed a fitness test and Asif Masood came in. The Australians chose to bat first, despite the overcast skies and heavy atmosphere — that just showed what they thought of our seamers. They were correct in their assessment, because we bowled very badly in such helpful conditions. The ball swung a great deal but I just couldn't control it and with each successive over, I felt under extra pressure because I was letting the team down. I finished with 0 for 115 in Australia's total of 517 for 8 declared. Looking back on it all now, I would love to bowl on that Melbourne wicket again — it was seaming and swinging all over the place, and I didn't know whether to go flat out and risk wasting the new ball or slow down, pitch the ball up and try to control the swing. In the end, I fell between two stools and was hopeless. At one stage in our first innings we were 241 for 1, but Lillee tumbled us out for 333, even though the wicket got easier. It was one of the finest spells I've seen in Test cricket, despite our poor middle order batting. So we had virtually lost the match when the Australians batted again, intent on quick runs so they could get at our batsmen again. That second innings was one of the major turning points in my bowling career. I had been so disappointed with my efforts so far on the tour that I vowed to go out and risk being taken apart. In the absence of Sarfraz, I was the main strike bowler in the team, so I gave it my all. After all, I had been thrashed while striving for line and length in the first innings, so I had nothing to lose. The conditions were easier for batting but in the absence of cloud cover, I somehow found it easier to control my swing and length. I managed to hit on the off-stump line and felt aggressive towards the batsmen, rather than just taking a hammering lying down. Greg Chappell miscued a hook; the ball coming much quicker than he expected. Then I gave Rodney Marsh a fright with a bouncer that hit him on the forehead. 'Where did you get that extra yard of pace from?' he asked me, shrugging off the blow. It's funny how such insignificant remarks have such significant effects: after that innings, I was an authentic fast bowler in my eyes. It had all come together and I would spend the rest of the tour striving to regain that rhythm and control. I finished with 5 for 122. I was driven to all-out attack by my own desperation and the fact that the match was out of our control — sure enough, we collapsed tamely in the second innings and lost by 348 runs.

This was the first time I had been with a Pakistan team that had lost a Test and the manner of defeat was chastening. We also had to take some strong comments from the Australian crowd in the field during the Test. Our manager, Colonel Shujauddin was to blame for that. He had said publicly that Lillee was out of order to have written off Pakistan in his newspaper column; furthermore, since two of the team had been to Oxbridge (Majid and myself), we were far better qualified to write columns in the press. Majid and I were terribly embarrassed at this remark, which inferred that the Australians were semi-literate.

As we prepared for the final Test, the match against Queensland proved to be a significant one for me. I took five wickets in the game and bowled faster than at any previous time in my career. Admittedly, the Brisbane wicket was fast, but I got into such a good rhythm that my confidence was boosted immensely. I bumped into Geoff Boycott at Brisbane and he gave me some good advice: he said that I must bowl fast in Australia when the ball is hard and new, because it soons gets soft and the batsmen then flourish when the shine has worn off. He said I definitely had the capacity to bowl fast, and I set out to prove him right.

I had decided that fitness was to be a crucial element in my efforts to be a fast bowler at the highest level, so I doubled up on my training programme before the final Test. To me the issue was a simple one, I wouldn't be able to concentrate fully on my bowling if dogged by fatigue. I had to be supremely fit. When we arrived at Sydney, we were all determined to avenge the humiliation at Melbourne and not even Lillee's familiar war of words — 'at last I've found a wicket to suit me' — managed to upset us. Chappell showed his contempt for our opening bowlers by choosing to bat on a humid day on a wicket that would help the seamers if they bowled properly. This time we did bowl correctly; Sarfraz and I took nine wickets and they were dismissed for 211. I must admit I was favoured by brilliant catching and some panic by the batsmen, but at least I bowled fast in long spells and sultry weather and again dismissed Chappell with a lifting leg-cutter.

At last our batsmen buckled down to the task and gave us a lead of nearly 150. When we bowled again, Mushtaq threw the ball to me ahead of Sarfraz; I stole a look at my opening partner, wondering if he had seen any significance in the move. He was not happy, but that only reflected his competitive spirit. As far as I was concerned, Mushtaq now saw me as his front-line strike bowler and I would do my best to keep up that standard. Sarfraz and I proceeded to bowl almost all day in sultry conditions but my extra training had paid off. I managed to get a lot of bounce from the wicket and several of their batsmen got out to the hook shot against my bouncers. My reward was twelve wickets in the match and we won by eight wickets — a memorable day for myself and the team. I must admit that subsequently I have bowled better for less reward, but our fielding was so brilliant that it inspired the bowlers. When Alan Davidson presented me with the Man of the Match award, he said it was one of the most outstanding feats he had seen on the Sydney Cricket Ground — a slight exaggeration, I felt, but nevertheless all very pleasant to hear. To my intense embarrassment, favourable comparisons were being made between the pace of Lillee and myself — a travesty and an insult to a great bowler — but I must admit I felt very good in that Test. The outfield is so marvellously smooth at Sydney that a fast bowler is never troubled by bumps and undulations as he sprints up to the wicket. So I got quickly into rhythm and felt very much in control. In those days, I relied heavily on rhythm in my run-up, much more than I do now. If I struggled to run up properly, my bowling would look very ordinary indeed. At Sydney that day, it all fell into place as I bowled non-stop for almost four hours. I even tore my shirt sleeve off my bowling arm through striving for extra effort!

That tour ended too soon for us. We had attained respectability in the eyes of the Australian team and public — there was even talk of an extra Test, but it couldn't be fitted into our crowded itinerary. I was an overnight sensation after winning the Sydney Test, finding myself deluged with offers to play grade cricket for vast sums of money. Test cricket was still the ultimate for me, however, and I wished that Pakistan's image had been higher in the eyes of the world's administrators at that time. We deserved a five-Test series in Australia, yet we had to be shoe-horned into a series lasting just three weeks. Like New Zealand, we seemed to be fitted in at the convenience of the major cricket countries — surely Pakistan was now in that bracket?

That point was underlined when we toured West Indies immediately afterwards. They had won the World Cup and thrashed England 3–0 in the last eighteen months, and yet we matched them all the way, except in seam bowling. Although I took 25 wickets in the series, Garner, Croft and Roberts took 77 between them. As soon as I arrived in the West Indies, I realised the folly of the comparisons between Lillee and myself. In the Caribbean, a club bowler is quicker than the fastest from Pakistan, and I also took my time to find a proper rhythm. The great Sir Gary Sobers took one look at me and announced dismissively: 'If he's as quick as Lillee, then Lillee must've been bowling at half pace!'

West Indies was quite a contrast to Australia. The wickets were much slower, and the facilities at the Test ground were far inferior. Yet away from the cricket, life was idyllic with wonderful sandy beaches, the joyous steel bands and large, luxurious hotels. At last we had plenty of time to get acclimatised before the series started. Time enough for Zaheer to fracture his toe, courtesy of an over-exuberant Javed Miandad while playing beach volleyball, an injury that kept him out of the first two Tests. Nevertheless, on paper we had plenty of batting re-inforcements, even if they invariably proved brittle throughout the series.

The first Test at Bridgetown was one of the best I've ever played in; fortunes changed so dramatically that it was impossible to back the winner right till the end. On the last day, they needed 306 to win and at 142 for 1 they were in charge. Then they panicked after being frustrated by some tight bowling. At 217 for 8, we had another fifteen minutes plus twenty overs to get two more wickets but Andy Roberts batted ninety minutes for 9 not out, Holder forty-five minutes for 6 and Croft — in his first Test — lasted out for the final eight overs. It was ironic that Holder and Roberts were two of the three men who had thwarted us in that astonishing game at Edgbaston in the 1975 World Cup — after winning that match against all odds, they were now hanging on here for a draw. We lost our heads in that last hour, Mushtaq kept chopping and changing the bowlers without giving them time to settle. He used the leg-spin of the inexperienced, excitable Javed, yet didn't bowl himself; his variety, flight and googly would surely have been too much for tail-enders who were just trying to survive.

My bowling in that Test was unimpressive. My five wickets in the match cost forty runs apiece, and that was no more than I deserved. Certainly Sarfraz and I had a tough task against the West Indian batsmen. Their first four in the order were incredibly talented — Fredericks and Greenidge would start the innings as if the seam had to be detached from the ball as quickly as possible, then Richards and Lloyd would carry on the slaughter. Fredericks was a fluent timer of the ball while Greenidge was a butcher and at his peak. Subsequently he looked a little unhappy against high pace but in this series, he was all power and confidence. He could also play sensibly when the state of the game needed this. Clive Lloyd was a terrific striker of the ball but I felt more optimistic when bowling at him than the others. My ability to bowl the inswinger to the right-hander meant that left-handers like Lloyd would be vulnerable if the ball left him late. Somehow Fredericks, another left-hander, was better at leaving the ball than Lloyd. My first encounter with Richards was an interesting test of psychological wills; for some reason he was very hostile to me. At various stages, he would sneer and glance sharply at me, and when I appealed for an lbw that must have been very close, he said: 'I'll come down there and shove this bat down your throat'. I was rather perplexed at that, because I was under the impression that only bowlers did the swearing! Any efforts at retaliation with bouncers were immediately hooked with ease to the boundary. By the end of the series, we had developed some sort of mutual respect — I had dismissed him four times, by bowling sensibly at him. I wish I had been so sensible when my side needed some coolness in the second Test. We had been bowled out on a wet wicket for 180 and with Sarfraz ruled out through injury, the responsibility for an early break-through was squarely on my shoulders. I bowled appallingly, losing my temper when hit around the field, and failing to control my line and length. Eventually Mushtaq couldn't afford the luxury of my bowling and I wasn't brought back until the end of the innings when our spinners were being smashed around. Luckily I managed to retrieve some self-respect in the second innings, though not in time to save the game. They needed 206 to win and on the final morning, the target was just over 60 with nine wickets in hand. I proceeded to bowl one of the finest spells of my Test career — I managed to swing the ball and ran in comfortably. The result was swing bowling at speed. I got 3 for 10 in a ten over spell that included the wickets of Greenidge and Richards. Then Wasim Bari dropped Kallicharran off me just after he'd come in, with the West Indies still 30 adrift and looking very jumpy. If only our inconsistent batting had held firm! If only I had bowled better in that first innings!

At least we managed to display the right kind of fighting spirit in the next Test. They led us by 250 in the first innings and we had to bat through the last two days to stave off defeat. We made over 500 and managed a draw fairly comfortably. We were indebted to a remarkable 167 from Majid; what was even more astonishing was his forecast that he was going out there to play just that kind of innings. That was very unlike Majid to tempt fate in such a way; he said he was going to punish Croft for his recent successes and he did just that in thrilling fashion. If Majid prospered at Georgetown, his opening partner picked up a significant injury. Sadiq was hit on the jaw as he tried to hook Roberts and he was badly shaken. I believe he was never the same batsman again. His arrogance against fast bowling had gone for ever, a point I noticed whenever I bowled subsequently at him in county cricket. Sadiq suffered the same fate as every batsman I have known, with the exception of Viv

Richards: at some point in their careers, they get ruffled by the fast men. Some get over it, others never do. It was just our luck that the injury to Sadiq affected him so much, because he and Majid were then the best opening pair in the world, apart from Fredericks and Greenidge.

Despite the brilliance of Fredericks and Greenidge, we remained convinced that the West Indies batting was rather vulnerable once the first three had been prised out. The fourth Test proved us right; they declined from 73 for 0 to 154 all out in the first innings and then they were bowled out for 222, to give us victory by 266 runs. My first innings effort pleased me; 4 for 64, including the wickets of Lloyd, Fredericks and Richards. I kept up my pace and managed to control the swing. So everything was set up for the decisive final Test at Sabina Park. The wicket was true and unusually fast and I enjoyed myself with the extra bounce. Unfortunately, the heat was so intense that I felt totally drained after six overs. It was an exhausting, clammy heat that drained me of all energy; at the end of an exacting tour, this was the worst time to be affected by such conditions. My socks were drenched with sweat and when I ran into bowl, my boots sounded as if I'd put my feet in a bucket of water! Although I took 6 for 90, I would've been even more successful if fatigue hadn't taken its toll. Gordon Greenidge also played one of the greatest Test innings of my time: exactly 100 out of 280. Not only did he shield the other batsmen from me, but he took me apart with some magnificent shots.

Nevertheless, we were in a strong position when we started our reply. Just four fast overs from Andy Roberts altered the psychological balance: he was at his quickest and most dangerous. He shook up Majid rather badly and this was a major blow to our confidence because Majid had looked masterful throughout the tour and we had come to rely greatly on him. Mushtaq had been worked over by Lillee and hadn't really recovered from the bouncer barrage in Australia while his brother, Sadiq was still uncomfortable after being hit on the jaw by Roberts at Georgetown. Judging by the looks on our team's faces at close of play we had lost that Test. We had been touring for over four months and no longer were we functioning at our peak. Roberts had wrested the initiative away from us with just a few fast deliveries, even though the other bowlers took the bulk of the wickets. Wasim Bari had to retire hurt after being hit in the face, hooking at Croft, and he missed out on his wicket-keeping duties on the next day when West Indies batted again. That seemed to depress us further and the West Indies carved out a big lead. Towards the end of their innings, Sarfraz and I decided to give a liberal helping of bouncers to Roberts, Garner and Croft, on the assumption that we would get a few when we batted. We were not mistaken.

We needed 442 to win and Mushtaq and I faced some frightening bouncers. Mushtaq received the treatment because he had said on television that he thought Roberts and Garner threw the ball; to say the least, they were displeased at the allegation and Mushtaq got some horrifying bouncers, which did nothing for his confidence that was already wafer-thin. When I walked out to bat, I knew I was heading for some rough weather. The crowd hadn't forgotten my bouncers and chanted 'blood, blood' as I took guard. I was still fairly confident about my ability to play the hook shot and I fended off the first ball from just in front of my nose. The next ball was the quickest I have ever faced — it was a bouncer and I was still halfway through my shot when it whizzed past my left ear and almost cleared the wicket-keeper. An inch or two the other way and I would have been killed. I would not have been able to avoid it. Thereafter I avoided hooking Roberts and when batsmen started wearing helmets a year later, I had no qualms about doing the same. Although we lost easily enough, our faces were saved by a truly remarkable innings from Asif Iqbal. He scored 135 in a dazzling exhibition of scintillating strokeplay. I would have described it as the innings of a lifetime were it not for the fact that he had already played two similar knocks on that tour in Tests. At Adelaide, he made 152 not out, which included an astonishing display of assurance during a last-wicket stand of 87 with Iqbal Qasim. Asif manipulated the strike so superbly that Iqbal Qasim only made four! His 120 at Sydney also came during a crisis and he helped give us an invaluable lead. He had started his rich vein of form with 166 against New Zealand just before we left for Australia, and from that day until he retired from Test cricket in 1979, he was our best batsman along with Majid. He seemed to revel in 'do-or-die' situations, where the only alternative was to play his shots or succumb tamely. Asif got into position so quickly and he was a great improviser. He could cut very late and with complete control, and in the later stages of his Test career he played straighter. Before he seemed to have almost too many shots but between 1976 and 1979, he curtailed his array of strokes but still played them magnificently. I never saw a better batsman when he had the tail-enders to protect: his running between the wickets would invariably conjure up a crucial single from somewhere, and he was so calm in such situations.

So we lost the West Indies series narrowly, but gained many new admirers in the process. I believe we should have beaten them, because the slow wickets suited our batsmen. Unfortunately our batting rarely functioned at full throttle throughout that long tour. On paper we batted in far greater depth than either of our opponents, yet consistency eluded us. I was disappointed with my batting efforts; too often I played a rash shot. I believe that our bowlers made much more out of their resources than our richly talented batsmen, a perennial problem with Pakistan Test sides. Without the chance to learn how to bat under pressure in domestic cricket, our batting folded up too often when men like Lillee, Roberts and Croft turned the screw. There almost seemed to be a subconscious feeling that the other batsmen could come up with the goods if some failed: no one really took responsibility. If we had been more experienced tourists at that time, I believe the extra big-match experience would have seen us win both series. Certainly our fielding was superior to that of Australia and West Indies.

If Mushtaq had been more decisive as a captain, I believe we might have fared better. Although full of aggressive ideas, he became rather too cautious for my liking as the tour progressed. He wanted to pack the side with batting and sometimes misread the pitch. When we won the Sydney Test, Mushtaq received a lot of credit, but I think the team he had selected was very ill-balanced. The pitch looked to be helping seamers — as events turned out, this was correct — yet he went into the match with just two seamers plus a slow left-armer, and relied on Asif Iqbal's gentle medium pace as third seamer. Sarfraz and I just had to keep bowling throughout the day and we took eighteen of the twenty wickets to fall. If the Australians had been able to build a big partnership in Sydney, we would have been in trouble, because there was no seam bowling back-up.

Sarfraz had great difficulty in reaching an understanding with Mushtaq on the field. He was distrusted by the team for his unorthodox and unpredictable views, yet on that 1976/77 tour I discovered Sarfraz's great cricketing brain. In the first Test at Barbados, we had a chance of a substantial lead after reducing them to 183 for 5 in reply to our 435. Clive Lloyd was the only recognised batsman left. Sarfraz was bowling beautifully, swinging the old ball and tying down the batsmen. The new ball was due and Mushtaq wanted to take it, but Sarfraz came up to me and said, 'Please tell Mushy not to take the new ball, he doesn't listen to me.' Sarfraz knew that the new ball wouldn't swing in controlled fashion when both sides of it were shiny and that it would come onto the bat with ease. I could see his line of reasoning and I passed my views on to the captain. He ignored us, took the new ball and Lloyd tore into us. He and Murray added 151, Lloyd scored 157 and they finished just 14 runs behind us. Sarfraz understood more on the art of seam and swing bowling than anyone on either side, yet Mushtaq thought he knew best — he would use the phraseology of English county captains about 'pitching the ball up and let it do the work', without realising that if the ball wasn't going to swing or seam, just pitching it up to the West Indian batsmen was courting disaster.

Listening to Sarfraz on that tour was the first time I thought an opening bowler could be captain, because he understood things about seam and swing bowling that Mushtaq couldn't possibly comprehend. For the rest of the trip Mushtaq used to joke that our seamers were the only ones in the world who never wanted a new ball which only proved he had missed the point of that Barbados experience. There were times when the new ball was a godsend, yet other times when it complicated matters.

In April 1977 the reputation of Pakistan stood high in the cricket world, despite our human frailties. Most of our batsmen were still at their peak (Majid, Asif, Zaheer and Wasim Raja), our reserves were good (Haroon Rashid and Javed Miandad) and talented young batsmen like Mudassar Nazar and Mohsin Khan were on their way to Test standard. Sarfraz and myself lacked a little support in the seam bowling department, but we had proved our mettle at home and abroad. In my opinion Wasim Bari was at this time the best wicket-keeper in the world. It was such a shame that this Pakistan side didn't play together for another eighteen months, due to the Packer problem. By then, some had passed their peak. I believe we would have fared very well on the 1978 England tour, but that wasn't to be.

As for myself, I was reasonably happy with my bowling during the three Test series of 1976/77. I had taken 57 wickets in eleven Tests and fared well against some of the world's best batsmen. My batting had languished, but for the moment, it seemed my main value to the side was as a strike bowler. Once and for all I had decided that my strength lay in my bowling, not my batting. Now I had to improve my bowling to survive at the highest level.

6 Cricket with Kerry Packer

My two years with World Series Cricket turned me into an infinitely better fast bowler. When I signed in April 1977, I was still fairly raw, able to generate pace at times but with a predominant inswing and an over-reliance on the bouncer. By April 1979, I had more or less got it right — I was getting closer to the stumps, which made me more side-on at delivery, enabling me to move the ball away from the bat. I now used more discretion with the bouncer and had more variety.

In county cricket during that period, I experimented most of the time with minor alterations to my action. I went round the wicket, which helped me stand up straighter at the moment of delivery to avoid falling in front of the umpire's line of vision. Previously, I'd had a tendency to fall away in delivering from over the wicket, with a resulting loss of control. Now my action was stabilised and my run-up smooth. I felt more confident of putting the ball where I wanted it.

Without World Series Cricket, I probably would never have been able to improve so dramatically. It gave me the chance to observe at close quarters the classical bowling styles of men like Lillee, Snow, Roberts and Holding and to analyse why they were great technical performers. The superb quality of the Channel 9 coverage also allowed me to dissect my action, thanks to those excellent close-ups and slow motion sequences. I would sit for long periods, watching where my feet landed at the crease, examining the position of my body at the point of delivery. The competition for places in the World XI was so intense that I just had to improve, otherwise I would be an also-ran. I was lucky to have the advice and support of two great fast bowlers, John Snow and Mike Procter. I respected their achievements and was gratified to discover that they were ready to offer advice and encouragement. I still had an inferiority complex about appearing alongside so many great fast bowlers, knowing that I still had much to learn, despite my encouraging performances in Tests. Procter worked on my run-up, telling me I must make it more fluent and less of a strain, while Snow emphasised the necessity of getting side-on and closer to the stumps, thereby making the inswinger more effective. Snow told me that it took him a long time to get into the side-on habit; in his early days, he used to be open-chested. I was determined to do the same and the first signs that I was achieving this came in the English season of 1978. I tore a side muscle when bowling — it was very painful, but the consolation was that it had resulted through my attempts to get side-on. The injury convinced me that my action was changing for the better; I then had to toughen up the muscles that hadn't been stretched very much in my old action.

Although my performances in the first year of WSC were unimpressive, I nevertheless found it an exhilarating experience. The tremendous coverage on Channel 9 brought the game to an entirely new audience. Packer really sold cricket and he personalised the players by endless close-ups and exaggerating their cricket prowess. Derek Underwood might be shown bowling in a Test, as a voice stated 'Deadly Derek loves a sticky wicket', while Michael Holding's beautiful run-up and delivery would be displayed in slow motion. Young people came to relate more and more to WSC — they started up fan clubs for the players and gave vociferous support during the games. They loved to see bouncers and with so many quick bowlers around, they weren't disappointed. I couldn't understand the traditionalists moaning about the dominance of fast bowling. To me it was the most exciting cricket I'd seen, great fast bowlers up against aggressive batsmen. I remember Mick Jagger once describing how he got interested in cricket: it was the sight of Dennis Lillee roaring up in his full glory. I had felt the same way about Lillee.

The quantity and quality of fast bowling inevitably brought problems to the batsmen. Most of them were hit at some stage and the worst injury was to David Hookes, who had his jaw broken in three places by Andy Roberts. Ashley Mallett ducked into one of my bouncers and spent a week in hospital. I was hit on the neck and was lucky to escape with just a bruise. That element of danger appealed to the crowd: guts is a crucial ingredient in ability and it takes a lot to stand there and battle through a bouncer barrage. Packer realised that the public loved that gladiatorial atmosphere, so it was up to the players to defend themselves. The protective helmet became the fashion, and not before time. A batsman cannot help himself when his confidence against fast bowling starts to ebb away; I remember being affected once when I was practising at the Lahore Gymnkhana and I was hit lightly on my cheek. It didn't hurt that much but shortly afterwards when I played in a match, I found myself instinctively taking my eyes off short-pitched deliveries. I needed a lot of practice and a few innings before I could start looking at the ball again when it was pitched short. For a time in the seventies, Aftab Baloch was blossoming into one of the most devastating batsmen in Pakistan: he hit 428 in one first-class match and to me he looked a genius. Once he was hit on the head, his confidence was shattered and he was never the same player again. In such situations, the players' grapevine gets to work and the shell-shocked batsman gets a large quota of bouncers. Either he comes out of it or he disappears from the scene.

One player in World Series Cricket had come through that ordeal and my admiration for him was immense. Ian Chappell had been sorely troubled by Mike Procter, Peter Pollock and John Snow in a twelve-month period in 1970 and he looked very suspect against the quicks for a time. However he battled to overcome his problem and became a magnificent Test batsman, a man for the crisis. In WSC he played some amazingly gutsy innings, especially one against the World XI in the Super Test Final. Australia were following on and had no chance of saving the match when Chappell came in at number three. Straight away, Andy Roberts hit him on the hand and broke it; he refused to come off and stood there batting one-handed for an hour. Chappell inspired the other batsmen, and made them fight with the same sort of guts and determination. No wonder he was such a great captain — his team would follow him anywhere because he led by example and expected others to reach his standard. Australian cricket was in the doldrums when he was appointed captain and he shook it up, moulded the team into a fighting unit so that they became the best in the world for about five years. I rated Chappell a better captain and batsman than his brother, Greg. Greg was more elegant, yet he didn't play the bouncing ball as well. He seemed to get onto the front foot a little too early. Players who like to drive don't play the short-pitched stuff that well, Viv Richards is the only exception. Nevertheless Greg Chappell is a superb player on slow wickets, a fine timer of the ball, and has a great Test record.

Viv Richards was head and shoulders above all the batsmen in WSC and he remains the best player at whom I have ever bowled. The bouncers were wasted on him for he had reflexes like a gunslinger and he was quick enough to hook off the front foot. He didn't bother with a helmet, relying on his superb eye to get him out of trouble. Over the years the best way to get him out is by boring him:

he'll race to his fifty, then chafe when the field is placed in defensive positions. He'll sometimes get frustrated by just taking singles and do something rash. Yet when his side really needs a big innings, Richards is there. A man for a crisis. Of course he plays across the line and you think you've got a chance, but he can hit the ball virtually in any part of the field because he gets into position so quickly.

The other Richards also looked high class in World Series Cricket. From what I saw of him there, and in county cricket, Barry Richards was a wonderful player. Technically he was the most correct batsman of my time and his balance and gift of timing were faultless. I remember an amazing innings of 200 he played for the World XI against the Australians, where he simply toyed with all the bowlers, and placed the ball disdainfully through the gaps.

The most dynamic cricketer in the World Series games was undoubtedly Dennis Lillee. I thought he was a tremendous bowler and entertainer and I believe he's done more for cricket throughout the world than anyone else in the past decade. He was a trump card for any television boss and the crowd loved him. He once told me he was at his peak during World Series Cricket, because he had to bowl at his best for so long against so many great batsmen. From the day I first saw him in 1972, he's been the best bowler of my era. He had so many injury problems, but he's always battled through them. He fights all the time, never shirks responsibility: he came to Pakistan in 1980 and took just three wickets in three Tests, but he bowled his heart out, trying every tactic and keeping up his aggression. That's the sign of fast bowling greatness — when it's hot, the wicket is slow and your side needs a breakthrough. Unlike Andy Roberts, Michael Holding and John Snow, great bowlers who sometimes needed to be cajoled, Dennis Lillee never gave up, but made things happen by sheer will-power. With a superb action, he was really quick for a long time and he was great in a crisis when he simply had to get wickets for his side.

With men like Lillee around, there was never any doubt that World Series Cricket was ulta-competitive. Our detractors tried to suggest that some of the games were fixed, which was total nonsense. Every game was fiercely competed; it was quite a contrast to a Test tour, where the pressure is eased when playing against a State or a county side. In WSC, there were no easy games — you were either bowling at Viv Richards and Clive Lloyd or the Chappells, then batting against Andy Roberts or Dennis Lillee. Any player of self-respect would want to give his all in such illustrious company. My only criticism was the gruelling itinerary.

During that first year of World Series Cricket, Mushtaq, Zaheer and I were led to believe that we now had permission from the Board to fly back to Pakistan to play in a Test against England. I was overwhelmed at the prospect, because I still had great regrets at missing out on the England series. I was finding WSC an enthralling challenge, but to me, nothing could surpass Test cricket. The man responsible for the alleged compromise between the Board and Kerry Packer was Omar Querishi, the well-known Pakistan cricket commentator: he claimed to have the authority of the President to negotiate for our release to play in the final Test at Karachi. Previously the Board had refused to talk to Packer; they were rather pleased that at last the undesirable element had been weeded out. Packer was delighted at the change of heart, feeling that it was a major breakthrough to be on terms of negotiation with one of the Test countries, and he agreed to our temporary release. Asif Iqbal didn't want to go, because he said he'd already retired from Test cricket, while Majid Khan's wife Seema was ill — that left Zaheer, Mushtaq and myself. We flew home, excited at the prospect of playing again for our country. We were soon in for some shocks.

No one knew we were on our way. No official was waiting for us at Karachi Airport. Mushtaq and Zaheer went to their respective homes and I was left stranded at a late hour, wondering what was going on. I found out the next day. I arrived at the Karachi Stadium, to see Zaheer and Mushtaq wandering around, looking rather lost. After a time we changed into our whites and reported to the selectors: they greeted us with a mixture of hostility, surprise and amusement that we thought we were going to play. After a brief discussion, they told us rather reluctantly to join in the net practice. For the first time in my life I wanted a cricket field to open up and swallow me; all the officials and some of the players made us feel distinctly unwanted. In our foolishness, we honestly thought we'd be welcomed back with open arms to strengthen the side. Instead we were greeted by the captain, Wasim Bari in this way: 'Who invited you here? Who said you were playing?' The atmosphere was rather chilly and we were relieved when we were called in front of the chairman of the selectors, Mohammad Hussain. After being locked in consultation with the leading Board officials, he calmly told us that we could play in the Test if we denounced our WSC contracts. We were dumbfounded: we pointed out that Omar Querishi had been negotiating with Kerry Packer, only to be told that Querishi had no authority and had nothing to do with the Board. I had suffered financially for wanting to play for my country, I was the only Pakistani to be selected for the Super Test back in Australia, so I missed out on five thousand dollars to fly home, only to be humiliated. Perhaps the Board had capitulated under pressure from the England players. On the eve of the Karachi Test, the England squad threatened to pull out if the three Packer men were reinstated. I thought that was an unwise attitude: what had it to do with them? That kind of official threat should have come from their employers at Lord's. They would have been in great trouble if they'd refused to play against us because no touring team can influence local selection.

My feelings can well be imagined as I watched Pakistan being overwhelmed in England in 1978. The wickets and the wet weather were against them and I am sure the Packer repercussions took their toll.

It was frustrating for me; I was banned because of my Packer connections, yet three who were also involved were playing in the tests — Javed Miandad, Sarfraz and Haroon Rashid. A further irony was that my form was so good, especially with the bat; while Pakistan lost by an innings in the first Test, Zaheer and I scored 213 and 167 respectively in a county match at the same time.

By the time I returned to Australia for the second year of World Series Cricket, peace was on the horizon. We had played in the Test series against India and although Packer and the cricket Establishment still seemed poles apart, at least informal discussions were taking place discreetly and there seemed less chance of the illogicalities of the previous year. I was happier about my long-term prospects and my form in that second year was better. I received a welcome boost to my confidence by coming third in a fast bowling contest, even though I had barely recovered from jet-lag. Twelve of the fastest WSC bowlers were involved: each of us delivered eight balls and our speed was measured. Michael Holding was second and Jeff Thomson came out on top — an irony for me, considering that in my early days, my action had been rather similar to that of Thomson. He looked very well co-ordinated and impressively fast during that competition, but I must admit I was glad I had changed from such a javelin thrower's style of bowling, with that kind of action it's almost impossible to do anything other than just bowl fast, rather than try for seam and swing.

Although Thomson was electronically quicker on that day, I still don't believe that anyone has been consistently quicker than Michael Holding during my time in the game. He is the only one I've batted against who regularly bowled very fast; he makes the ball bounce from very near the bat, so you don't know whether to duck or stand there and play it. He has the best run-up and action of any fast bowler I have seen, and although he doesn't seem to think all that much about his bowling, I suppose that isn't necessary with such speed. He lacks Lillee's determination to battle through when the chips are down and the wicket is unhelpful, but nevertheless he has been a classic fast bowler and great to watch.

That second year of World Series Cricket was a success. The crowds were larger, the cricket even tougher and more skilful and our brand of cricket was compared favourably to the traditional version (the Ashes series was being played in Australia at the same time). I bowled better and better as the season wore on, with my rhythm very good and I prospered with a new bowling partner in Garth le Roux. He bowled superbly and we were a good partnership: to my delight, he agreed to join Sussex a year later and we became a good combination in county cricket. It was a great thrill to play for a World XI containing so many fine bowlers. After our opening blast, there was Procter, Rice and Underwood. The batting was long and talented — Richards, Majid, Zaheer, Rice, Asif, Procter, Greig, Knott and myself. I didn't get much batting practice, shades of the Pakistan Test side! No wonder we won the Grand Final and the jackpot of 62,000 dollars.

By the end of World Series Cricket in 1979, many cricketing reputations had been made and broken. Some had been found wanting in the fiercely competitive nature of the game. My knowledge had been considerably broadened by rubbing shoulders with so many great cricketers. I suppose the most spectacular casualty on the field was Tony Greig: at the start of WSC, he was a recent England captain, with an excellent Test record as an all-rounder. Two years later, he looked completely demoralised — lengthy sessions at the nets had failed to halt the slump in his playing fortunes. He left Sussex during the 1978 season and the lack of regular county cricket made him rusty in the Packer games. His decline was gleefully trumpeted by many Australian players, particularly Lillee and Ian Chappell who felt that he had always been overrated and that he had made too much money out of the game in proportion to his talents. I couldn't agree with that as his record in Tests was very good, especially when England was in a tight corner. The way he took on Lillee and Thomson when they were blasting through the other batsmen in 1974–75 was brave and daring. He was a wonderful fielder in any position and I admired his positive captaincy. I'm only sorry that I had little chance to play for Sussex under his leadership, because his positive style suited my temperament and was one of the main reasons why I joined Sussex. Many resented Greig's fluency with words and his skill in dealing with the media but I feel that many of his forecasts have come true since he helped set up World Series Cricket in 1977. Certainly he was perfectly fair and honest with me when I was asked to sign for Packer and it was not Greig's fault that attitudes hardened on both sides and the world of cricket was thrown into turmoil for a couple of years.

On balance, I had few regrets about playing for Packer, except that I missed Test cricket — the acme of the game for me. Apart from that my cricket education had been rapidly accelerated.

7 The Historic Indian Series

Just before the start of the second season of World Series Cricket, Pakistan played a very significant Test series — significant both for my county and for me. After an interval of eighteen years and two wars, Pakistan and India resumed Test relations with each other. Our pleasure at this was deep, and our excitement at such a prospect intense. My sense of expectation was sharpened when the Government made it quite clear that the Packer players would be selected for the Indian series, I was back in the fold and what a series in which to return!

The players were really keyed up about the prospect of playing India after such a long time. I shall never forget a request from Sadiq and Zaheer right at the end of the 1978 English season. I was playing for Sussex against Gloucestershire and they both pleaded with me not to bowl any bouncers at them in case they were injured and forced to miss the Indian series. At that time, the Tests were two months away! Neither was taking any chances — playing against India was that important.

I had one or two things on my mind as the series approached. I had torn a side muscle at the end of the county season as I tried to get used to my new action and the injury took a long time to heal. It felt very strange to be unfit after such a long time of good fortune and I had recurring nightmares that I would not be able to bowl properly again. In the training camps as we prepared for the Indians I became more and more anxious. My injury needed rest, yet I was desperate to get fit. I felt the pressure from not only my injury but also because I was a Packer player. After Pakistan's disastrous tour of England, the general public feeling was that the Packer men would make all the difference and that our country's cricketing pride was to be restored. As the time drew nearer, I became more and more nervous. I wasn't dogged by fear of failure but lack of dazzling success was my main worry because the public expected so much. Yet I still couldn't bowl properly due to my side injury; even when I batted, the pain was intense as I tried to drive off the front foot. Just a week before the first Test, the injury eased, enabling me to play.

The build-up to that Test was incredible. The whole nation seemed to be talking about it, as the media beat the drum with massive previews and interviews with players. Our press had built up the Indian team, praising their famous spin bowlers to the skies, yet the papers felt the Packer players would tip the scales in our favour. Unfortunately the massive build-up led to anti-climax. The wicket at Faisalabad was dreadfully easy; all grass had been removed and it had been rolled so much that it shone brightly, and the groundsmen had ensured it wouldn't spin. There was nothing in it for any type of bowler and the result was a high-scoring draw. There was neither bounce nor seam in the pitch and, as it was so hot and dry, the ball didn't swing at all. After the shine had been worn away, it was out of the question to imagine dismissing a class batsman, to beat the bat was judged an achievement. Sarfraz and I tried our hardest for an early breakthrough, but in the end we opted for varying our length. We sent down a liberal amount of bouncers — not to hit them, or tempt them into hooking, but to stop the batsman from driving off the front foot. Anything pitched up was just an invitation to runs, so we tried to make it difficult for them. We both conceded over a hundred runs, but in the circumstances (71 overs between us) I thought we couldn't have done much else. Our captain, Mushtaq clearly didn't agree because he said in a television interview that I in particular had bowled too short. Unfortunately, Mushtaq again showed the lack of knowledge about fast bowling that he displayed eighteen months earlier in the West Indies. He didn't seem to understand that we were trying to frustrate their batsmen by short-pitched bowling and hoping they would make rash shots. I was disgruntled at this ill-informed criticism by my captain; with the burden of public anticipation weighing very heavily on my shoulders, I didn't need that extra pressure.

I practised and trained very hard indeed for the next Test at Lahore. The atmosphere was fantastic as we put India in on a grassy wicket on a humid, misty morning, ideal conditions for seam and swing bowling. My opening spell was very erratic: I was terribly tense through all the various pressures on me and the ball was swinging around like a boomerang. The batsmen hardly had to play a ball in my first four overs and I was at a loss to know what to do, particularly as it seemed to me that my captain was losing faith in my ability. I was now rated as a world-class bowler, yet here I was incapable of utilising conditions that should have been ideal for me. The pressure on me got greater but I got a lucky break when Chauhan played on to one that, for a change, was straight. I picked up four wickets, the Indians were bowled out cheaply and I breathed a little easier. I bowled 42 overs in the second innings as we managed to winkle India out in just enough time to set up a thrilling finish. We needed 126 in a hundred minutes and our experience of limited-over cricket in England stood us in good stead, with Majid, Zaheer and Asif steering us home with eight overs to spare.

The crowd loved that exciting chase for runs on the final day and the fact that it led to victory over India was even more delightful. That Lahore Test sparked off the cricket boom in Pakistan which has lasted till the present day.

For too long, the Pakistan public had been subjected to tedious cricket, stemming from dreadfully slow wickets and negative captaincy — the fact that our drawn series the previous year against England had been hailed as a triumph just shows our lack of ambition and expectation of victory. This attitude has been ingrained in Pakistan for a long time, the previous thirteen Tests between India and Pakistan had all been drawn. Victory on either side was a novelty and the public was ecstatic. When we followed it up with another dramatic victory in the Karachi Test, the whole nation was overwhelmed with cricket fever.

At Karachi we needed 164 to win in a hundred minutes and we reached the target with seven balls to spare, to win by eight wickets. To my great pleasure, I was promoted in the order to number four and enjoyed a lucky over to hit Bishen Bedi for two sixes and a four to settle the issue. Strangely enough the public only seemed to remember my sixes after the match and all those overs on the dead wicket weren't considered very special.

Overnight, I became a star in Pakistan. I was hailed as the match winner, which was a little unfair on some of my colleagues, and I was amazed by the adulation. The radio and television coverage of the series had been excellent and everyone seemed to stop work and tune in to the cricket. Having experienced the public passion for the game in Australia and the West Indies, I was very gratified to see such enthusiasm in Pakistan. Within a few days of the Karachi Test, most sports shops in Pakistan had sold out of cricket equipment, and posters of the players sprung up in bookstalls, airports and railway stations. The game was established in the rural areas, thanks to this series; due to television and radio, that enthusiasm has not waned.

The Indian tour party was received with great warmth and hospitality wherever they went in Pakistan, although the relationship between the two sides was never very friendly. The umpiring was not as good as I had hoped and at times both sides suffered. However both sides agreed that resumption of Tests was long overdue and the administrators wasted no time in organising regular series between the two countries. Club and colts sides also started to travel back and forth over the border. As a result the game of cricket in both countries received a welcome boost and I look back on that 1978 series with great affection after a nervous start.

The two dominant batsmen of that series were Zaheer Abbas and Sunil Gavaskar. Zaheer not only scored masses of runs, but the manner of execution was superb. He looked the complete stroke maker on the slow wickets of Pakistan and he destroyed the Indian spinners, who looked past their best. His timing and placement of shots were absolutely breathtaking and he rarely bothered to loft the ball. He looked so utterly safe and his improvised shots — whipping a ball on the off stump through the legside, for example — carried an air of inevitability about them. Our careers have run more or less parallel and I consider Zaheer the best attacking batsman in the world on slow wickets against spin and medium pace. Unlike Viv Richards, he doesn't get bored with piling up runs and he keeps the ball on the ground. He plays very close to his body at the moment of impact and his reach off the front foot is enormous. He played one of the best shots I've ever seen during a Test against India — he went to drive a ball from Kapil Dev that wasn't quite up to him, so he checked his shot and played a forward defensive shot. The ball rocketed through the covers to the boundary, even though he played it defensively, his timing was so much in tune. My main criticism of Zaheer is that he hasn't always got runs when Pakistan needed a sizeable contribution in a crisis; in that respect the Asif Iqbal of 1976/79 was more valuable to us. Zaheer has been suspect against real pace and on suspect wickets, the only great innings I've seen from him on a wet wicket was a hundred against Underwood at Gravesend on his first tour of England in 1971. No English player of the same age and lack of experience could have played like he did when making 274 in his first Test in England. His range of strokes, timing and concentration were wonderful. Yet that Edgbaston wicket was ideally suited to Zaheer's style and his apparent inability to battle it out on unfavourable wickets in pressure situations meant he cannot be ranked above Viv Richards and Ian Chappell.

Sunil Gavaskar impressed me greatly on that 1978 tour and has continued to do so ever since. He is he most compact player I've ever bowled to, playing near to his body with a straight bat and has the ability to make late adjustments — a great asset for an opening batsman against the moving ball. He was terribly difficult to dismiss after seeing off the new ball and like Zaheer he loved the flat Pakistan wickets. He might look a little worried when I bounced him, but as he didn't play the hook, he was unlikely to play any rash shots. He always seemed to know where his off-stump was, and his wide array of strokes meant he could easily keep the score moving in unspectacular fashion. His greatness lay in the fact that he knew his limitations; he was a more refined version of Geoff Boycott. Gavaskar was always there when his side needed him most: India have been involved in some exciting run chases in the last innings of Tests over the years when a target of 400 plus has looked daunting, but each time Gavaskar has played marvellously and brought his team either to victory or pretty close. His only flaw was against the quick bowlers bowling into his body when his lack of height would get him rather tucked up. He would sometimes be in trouble on wickets of uneven bounce because he didn't hook, and was loath to duck or leave the ball because of the unpredictability of the bounce; apart from that, a masterful batsman with a great temperament.

While my status as a Test all-rounder rose in that Indian

series, India blooded a young man who would eventually become a splendid opponent with both bat and ball. Kapil Dev was just nineteen when he first played against us, but he looked a very fine prospect. In years to come, the press would make much of our rivalry as all-rounders, but I have always felt we were different types of cricketer. With the bat, Kapil is a fine wristy player and a lovely clean striker of the ball, who loves to get on with it. He is a more talented batsman than I am, but I think I've become a more responsible player. I can stay at the wicket longer, partly due to the demands of captaincy, while Kapil always seems to play the same adventurous way, hitting the ball very hard indeed. As bowlers we are again contrasting; he is only really fast–medium, although he is fast by Indian standards. He bowls a very good line and length, with a sharp bouncer but he is not a genuine fast bowler. I feel that he has been over-bowled by India and is unlikely to get any better, whereas his potential as a batsman is vast. I admire immensely his attacking attitude, which has attracted many people towards cricket. He is a great trier who has done wonders for Indian cricket in just a few years.

Although we triumphed 2–0 in the historic series, I felt at the time that we had the lucky breaks. Some controversial umpiring decisions went our way at Lahore and Karachi. At Lahore on the last day, India were 406 for 4 with lunch just a quarter of an hour away when Viswanath was bowled for 83 by Mudassar, playing a very injudicious shot in the circumstances. They quickly declined to 465 all out, when just another hour of defiance from Viswanath would have saved the game. We were also lucky that the toss at Lahore was won by Mushtaq and that gave us the first bowl on a wicket that helped us and then rolled out easy-paced when we batted. Basically the reason for our two victories was that the Indians lacked the bowling resources to bowl us out twice on good wickets.

I couldn't help thinking that we would face sterner competition from India when we visited them a year later. They would surely re-think their bowling strategy, now that their famous slow bowlers had slipped into mediocrity and their massive crowds would give them great support. It gave me no pleasure at all to be proved right in my assessment.

8 1979: My Worst Year in Cricket

Every cricketer experiences one year when nothing seems
to go right and disappointments and disillusion are never
far away. That was my lot throughout the year of 1979. It
began with a series in New Zealand marred by poor
umpiring, unsporting wickets and a profound lack of
atmosphere. Straight after that, we played two Tests in
Australia that were full of ill-feeling stemming from the
discord over World Series Cricket in which we stood to
lose everything and gain nothing. In these Tests, I
experienced a great sense of anti-climax after the enthralling Packer matches and I was appalled at several
unsportsmanlike actions of players from both sides. Three
months later, Pakistan again squandered two golden
opportunities in the second World Cup competition in
England, leading to two defeats that sickened me. Our
stock plummeted ever further when we went to India and
lost the series 2–0 through our own complacency over
team selection and lack of resilience under pressure. At
the start of 1979, Pakistan had been rated on a par with
Australia and the West Indies, with all the Packer players
recalled to the ranks, yet by the end of the year we were
on the bottom rung alongside New Zealand. It was so
galling and frustrating. In personal terms, I was downcast:
I didn't perform as well as I might at the highest level,
while my career in county cricket looked in jeopardy,
because Sussex seemed to have written me off.

Everything seemed so promising in those early weeks

of 1979. We all knew that something was in the air, which would allow the Packer players to return to full-time Test cricket and I couldn't wait to make an impact in a crowded year of Tests. I was happy with my revamped action and with all due modesty, I reasoned that my success in the second year of WSC should give me cause for optimism when representing Pakistan. Nothing could be tougher than the cricket I'd just played.

I arrived in New Zealand after my exertions in WSC to find us one up in the Test series with two to play. I missed the best game: Mushtaq and Wasim Raja bowled them out on the last day as they failed to reach a target of 305 by a wide margin. The wickets were slow, the weather rainy and much of the play was pointless as the matches headed for draws. It was such an anti-climax from the Packer games: I had to work very hard at motivating myself and although I was unlucky with some umpiring decisions, I was pleased with my haul of ten wickets in two Tests. In the second innings of the third Test, I bowled as well as I'd ever done in my Test career, yet managed only two wickets; the ball passed the bat regularly and when it was edged, someone dropped it.

The outstanding New Zealander was Richard Hadlee. He deservedly won the Man of the Series award, for his excellent, intelligent, seam bowling. Hadlee has been one of the best new-ball bowlers of my time, with a beautiful action giving him a superb outswinger that always troubles the right-hander. He has carried New Zealand for a long time and I can imagine how even more successful he would have been if playing for an established Test side. Like Pakistan, New Zealand haven't played all that many Tests until recently and their players have lacked experience in dealing with pressure situations. It's significant that they have started to improve as some of their best players get experience of English county cricket and play more Tests. If Richard Hadlee had been English, he would have taken 300 Test wickets by now.

If their players needed experience, the same applied to the New Zealand umpires. I thought the standard there was the poorest in the world. It was about this time that I started to believe that neutral umpires were the answer to the problem — three years before the subject was fully aired after some controversial incidents during our England tour.

The umpires were put under further pressure during our two-Test series in Australia immediately after the New Zealand trip. There was bad feeling between the sides throughout, and that led to three particularly regrettable incidents. At Melbourne, Javed Miandad ran out Rodney Hogg after the batsman had moved down the wicket to inspect the pitch following a defensive shot. Mushtaq tried to recall Hogg but the umpire refused and Hogg then smashed down his stumps before leaving the wicket. At Perth we looked as if we were going to save the match, thanks to a stubborn last-wicket stand by Asif and Sikander; Alan Hurst proceeded to run out Sikander as he backed up too eagerly as Hurst ran in to bowl. Asif then wrecked his own wicket in the same way as Hogg at Melbourne. In retaliation for the Sikander incident, Sarfraz appealed for 'handled ball' against Andrew Hilditch when the non-striking batsman picked up the ball after a fielder's return and handed it to the bowler. The appeal by Sarfraz was upheld and Hilditch had to go. Afterwards, Asif publicly deplored all three incidents, saying that wasn't the way to play cricket. He was right but forgot that he had contributed to the bad feeling by a foolish statement just before the first Test. Asif had said that the Australian team was sub-standard and that many of their players weren't good enough for Test cricket. This was true, but there was no need for Asif to say it in public, especially as he wasn't our captain. It put us under unnecessary pressure; this second eleven Australian team had just been hammered 5–1 by England. Pakistan, with all the Packer players back in the fold, would now be expected to be equally convincing. We should never have played those two Tests; the Australian Board fixed up the series just to deny Packer any further chance of televised cricket and both sets of players took up entrenched positions over the World Series Cricket issue. We only drew the series, but we were a much better outfit — yet we'd been playing almost non-stop for five months and the strain was telling.

We managed to win the first Test in extraordinary fashion. On the last day Australia needed just 77 for victory with seven wickets standing. An hour later, we had won: Sarfraz took seven wickets for just one run in the space of thirty-three deliveries and finished with an overall analysis of 9 for 86. The other wicket to fall was a run-out. At the other end, I had tried my hardest but couldn't make any impact. By tea-time, I had also strained back muscles trying to push myself into extra speed, so we needed something special to save our faces against a team we had publicly written off before the Test. Alan Border and Kim Hughes were playing superbly in a big partnership until Sarfraz bowled Border with a beautiful delivery that cut back off the seam. After that, it all fell into place for him and the Australians lost their nerve. On a slow, low wicket, Srafraz bowled in the right area and they collapsed from 305 for 3 to 310 all out.

It was typical of Sarfraz that he would come up with such an inspirational spell when he'd been having a pretty bad run. He hadn't looked at his best in New Zealand and some were saying that he was over the top but they reckoned without his capacity to surprise. He has been such a clever bowler over the years; I don't know of anyone who utilised the conditions so well. He may look ungainly in his run-up, but his action is balanced and side-on. He changes his action for different deliveries, uses the crease and cuts the ball either way off the pitch. He always seemed to know which ball would swing more than the others and as a result, Sarfraz would always make the choice when the umpires presented a box of new balls to us just before we went out on the field. He taught me more about swing bowling than anybody, disclosing little titbits to me as he got to know me a little better during our tours — that was something he refused to discuss with other bowlers. He has picked up Test wickets all over the world, despite having to bowl for long periods on dead wickets. I believe that he would have broken all Test bowling records if he had been English; at his peak (1972 to 76), he didn't play all that much for Pakistan, because we didn't have many Tests during that period. His achievement in taking a hundred championship wickets for Northants in 1975 was fantastic, considering that he missed a month through the World Cup and then had to bowl on those flat pitches at Northampton. Sarfraz is a bit of a loner and he has been at loggerheads with some players in our sides — notably Asif Iqbal — but I always felt he tried his best for the team. I've seen him carry injuries that would have sidelined less determined men, yet people allege that he pulls out of Tests because he doesn't fancy bowling on dead surfaces. That is nonsense; he never faked injuries and those who criticised him don't know the physical strain that a seam bowler is under, year in year out. He has always needed strong handling because he is a difficult person to handle. Sarfraz has a strong sense of self-preservation and many of his controversial actions have stemmed from a sense of insecurity. He is not one of the easiest of people to understand and get on with, yet some of my most enjoyable moments off the field have been spent with Sarfraz on overseas tours. He is extremely witty and articulate in Punjabi, a language I had never appreciated before meeting him, and he often sees the funny side of things. One of the greatest things I've learned from him is to forget about cricket as soon as the match is over and to unwind completely. I consider Sarfraz to have one of the best cricket brains of any cricketer I've known.

re bowling Imran always
stretches his back.

rking hard to keep fit.

Changing styles. *Left* before 1979 and open chested and *right* side on.

Imran in good form in the Gillette Cup, Sussex *v* Lancashire at Hove 1978.

Viv Richards is clean bowled by Imran, Melbourne 1981.

Becoming the highest wicket taker in Pakistan history; third Test, Melbourne 1981.

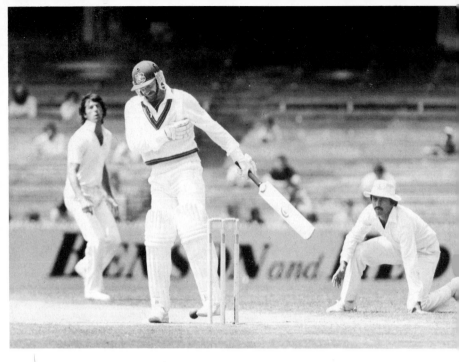

Intense rivalry on the field but friendly off it; Dennis Lillee falls victim to Imran in the third Test at Melbourne 1981.

Another Australian wicket; Bruce Yardley on this occasion.

The playboy image.

The jump that has transformed Imran's bowling.

In the second Test at Perth, we were desperately short of bowlers throughout. Mushtaq, thinking too defensively, packed the side with batting, leaving us with just three seamers and due to Mushtaq's injury, no spinners. I shouldn't have played (my back strain hadn't cleared up) and I had to have treatment during the intervals to keep me going. Worse was to follow, Sikander, our third seamer, pulled a muscle in his side and bowled just eleven overs in the match. That left Sarfraz and me to do most of the bowling, as my injury got progressively worse. We bowled 103 overs between us in the match, a convincing answer to those misguided critics who say that Sarfraz lacks heart. Our lack of bowling depth meant that Australia won comfortably by seven wickets.

I was terribly disappointed that we lost that Test. Our team selection was wrong, our fielding was very poor and although we were unlucky with injuries, that doesn't excuse our pathetic batting. We collapsed twice on an easy-paced pitch, and only high-class hundreds from Javed and Asif brought us some sort of respectability. Our attitude of mind was wrong, we were jaded. We had played ten Tests in five months, while some of us had been through a guelling time with World Series Cricket. Although fatigue was relevant, I felt there was something more substantially wrong with our side. My suspicions were confirmed in the World Cup a few months later.

The 1979 World Cup was a major tragedy for Pakistan because we lost two matches that we ought to have won. The trophy could so easily have been ours, but we were let down by a collective inability to cope with tension. This was the last time a fine Pakistan side that had been impressive for several years was together and we ought to have done ourselves justice before it began to break up.

The early signs were encouraging when we assembled in England. Our training went well and we destroyed county teams in practice matches. We brushed aside Australia in the first match at Nottingham. Australia were still ludicrously without their Packer players, even though Pakistan and West Indies played theirs. Nevertheless our performance was thoroughly professional in all departments and confidence in our camp was high. Our next game was against England at Leeds and we were favourites. It was to be a day of drama and eventual heartbreak for us.

The ground was packed at the start of play, with Pakistan enjoying vociferous support. The atmosphere was the sort that brings out the best in an international cricketer if his temperament matches his talent. The conditions favoured bowlers throughout and when England stood at 118 for 8, our supporters were delirious with joy. We then made our first blunder, allowing Willis and Taylor to add 43 precious runs. I felt our captain, Asif Iqbal, should have bowled me at Willis early on, but he thought that it was only a matter of time; certainly the batsmen made mistakes, but we failed to capitalise. Sikander dropped Willis and the ball kept disappearing to various parts of the ground from unorthodox shots. England eventually made 165 for 9 in their sixty overs — more than they should have got, but still well within the compass of our strong batting line-up.

We got away to a great start, with Majid and Sadiq opening with 27 in no time at all. Then Hendrick, in a classic display of seam bowling, reduced us to 34 for six. The familiar signs of panic in our batsmen were on display, but Asif played a beautifully controlled innings, with good support from Wasim Raja. I came in at 86 for 7, feeling very nervous. I decided to leave the shots to Asif and hold up an end; time was on our side, because England's main bowlers were nearing the end of their allotted overs. Gooch and Boycott would have to bowl and that's where the game could be won. Asif and I added 29 precious runs in an incredibly tense atmosphere: every run was wildly cheered by our supporters, while a maiden over was greeted with roars of approval by the

English. Asif and I were often beaten by unplayable deliveries pitched on a certain spot at Hendrick's end but we hung on. Just as we looked to be inching towards victory, Asif got an impossible ball from Willis that hit the ridge, and bounced nastily off the seam. In came Wasim Bari and he proceeded to play sensibly; Mike Brearley began to panic a little because he knew he would soon have to use his second-string bowlers. Quite rightly, he had gambled on bowling us out with his best bowlers, but now he would have to fiddle Boycott and Gooch through some testing overs. Only Willis was left to trouble us with three more overs. The score was 145 for 8, just 21 runs from victory and all we needed to do was pick up easy singles with plenty of overs left. At this stage, Wasim Bari played an exceptionally stupid shot, despite my exhortations — he tried to cut an inswinger from Boycott, who was bowling from round the wicket. Wasim was caught behind and the tension was now unbearable. Yet we could still win if the last man, Sikander did as he was told: I told him that we still had time on our side, that all he had to do was block Boycott and Gooch's gentle medium pace, and to leave the scoring to me. All the England field was ringed round the boundary edge when I was on strike, so I contented myself with singles for a time, convinced that I could launch an assault in the last two or three overs. I felt the pressure was likely to tell on the Engllish bowlers; Gooch and Boycott weren't regular bowlers and therefore likely to crack in the tension and send down some loose deliveries. We needed 15 to win with four overs left when the pressure got to Sikander who launched himself at a wide half-volley from Boycott and spooned up a catch to mid-off. I was left high and dry, 21 not out. I could have strangled Sikander at that moment, although he was miserable about his lapse of concentration. I had been grinding away for ages, steeling myself to be sensible and then all the hard work was thrown away in one rash shot. I could sympathise with

Sikander eventually; I had been guilty of many impetuous strokes in my time and if he had connected, the target would have then been only ten off four overs. The only consolation for me was that I had put up one of my best batting efforts of my career, even though I only scored 21.

We felt bad enough about the result, but our supporters were inconsolable. That night, many members of the immigrant community in Leeds let us know just how despondent they felt. It didn't matter that some of them knew very little about cricket, the important thing was that we had let victory over England slip from our hands. I had to be very self-controlled on occasions when asked why I hadn't hit out with just Sikander at the other end. There was no point in making any explanation of the field being placed on the boundary.

If the disappointment at Leeds was great, our despair at the Oval four days later was huge. We were very close to beating West Indies but threw it away through unprofessionalism. They had batted first on a flat Oval featherbed and slaughtered the quicker bowlers to make 293 for six. The wicket was so slow that the fast bowlers were completely nullified and with Roberts, Holding, Croft and Garner in the West Indies team, that was no bad thing for us. When Pakistan went in, we looked as if we were going to run away with the match and at one stage, we were 176 for 1, with Majid looking superb and Zaheer playing the best innings of the World Cup. The wicket was absolutely ideal for us with no pace to disconcert our batsmen and a huge outfield giving plenty of scope for runs. The West Indies bowling was in complete disarray and they were starting to argue with each other out in the middle. We needed just five an over to cruise home, with Majid and Zaheer looking unbeatable. I would have backed Sussex, or any decent county side to have strolled home from a similar position. When Zaheer was out to a freak dismissal, the game was still ours but Asif then made a fatal error. Instead of sending in Javed or himself, both with experience of one-day cricket and the appropriate tension, he sent in Harood Rashid, a man who had no experience of one-day cricket. Instead of simply tapping the ball and giving the strike to Majid, Haroon wasted valuable overs trying to find his bearings, stroking the ball to mid-off and getting no runs. The pressure built up and Majid got out forcing the pace. Even then Asif (the best player in such situations) didn't come in and Javed was out first ball. At last Asif entered with Pakistan on 187 for 4, still favourites to win with our depth of batting. Asif proceeded to play a most bizarre innings; he tried to hit Viv Richards for six and was dropped on the boundary, but when he tried it again, he was caught. It was an amazing effort from such an experienced cricketer who has played so many astonishingly calculated innings when overs are running out. Asif's next action shattered me; instead of putting me in to play some shots, he sent Mudassar Nazar in ahead of me. Now I have always been a great admirer of Mudassar, but in such circumstances he was surely the wrong choice — I had more strokes than a man who usually opened the innings and I also had experience of one-day cricket in England. By the time I got in, we were 220 for 6 and the innings just folded. We lost by 43 runs. West Indies proceeded to the final, where they beat England easily.

There was no excuse for losing at the Oval. Leeds was bad enough, but at least we had battled away and Hendrick had bowled superbly at us. The Leeds game had been more enjoyable, because the atmosphere was so tremendous — you could hear a pin drop at certain stages in our innings — but the Oval match was dreadfully disappointing. We simply capitulated under the pressure. Richards was the West Indies fill-in bowler with his undemanding off-breaks, yet he got three wickets! I began to wonder whether Pakistan had the character to win important matches in international cricket. My mind went back to Edgbaston 1975, when we should have beaten West Indies: it seemed they had a jinx on us. If we had triumphed at the Oval, I believe we would have won the World Cup, because England were the other finalists and I was sure we had the measure of them. They may have sneaked home at Leeds but surely we wouldn't have buckled again? Such thoughts were self-defeating; we were out of the World Cup through our own fault and our next opportunity to make amends was four years away, by which time most of our team would have been over the hill.

At the end of the season it became clear to me that Sussex were thinking of releasing me. There were now four overseas players on the books — Garth le Roux, Javed Miandad, Kepler Wessels and me — and although Javed Miandad left for Glamorgan, I felt that I was going to be the odd one out. Only two of the three could play at any one time and although Wessels made an impressive amount of runs, I believed that the team would benefit from a good opening bowling pairing. Le Roux and I had struck up a good relationship both on and off the field in World Series Cricket and I sincerely felt that we could win more matches for Sussex than a combination that included the batting of Wessels. Clearly Sussex disagreed with me and my prospects for the 1980 season looked bleak — at best I'd play in the one-day matches. My frustrations were understandable: I'd worked very hard indeed at my bowling action and it all started to come together in 1979. I topped the county bowling averages and averaged 35 with the bat and yet I was still unsure of my place for the following season!

I had little time to ponder my future with Sussex during the close season, as I launched myself into a six-Test series in India. It proved to be an exciting tour, played in front of vast, appreciative crowds, but for Pakistan it was a disaster and we lost the series two-nil with almost the same side that had triumphed a year earlier against the Indians. There is no doubt that India had improved: Gavaskar was a shrewd, unruffled captain, their fielding and catching were far better and Kapil Dev had advanced to world-class status as an all-rounder. They had a settled unit, playing the same eleven in the first four Tests. On the other hand, little went right for us: Sarfraz didn't tour because Asif was the captain and in general the team didn't pull together when the going was hard. Our batting was dreadful, with only Javed and Wasim Raja showing any consistency. The biggest disappointment was Zaheer who, after slaughtering the Indians a year earlier, declined spectacularly to average just nineteen. He was dropped for the last Test and it was clearly a relief to him. We were bowled out seven times in eleven innings, each for less than 300 and too often the occasion proved too much for batsmen who had surely picked up enough big-match experience to withstand the tension.

Our problems began right at the start of the tour with complacent team selections. Asif clearly thought our regular first eleven was sufficient and he gave little thought to the right reserves. Talat Mirza — who had only played under-nineteen cricket and a handful of first class matches — was taken. Sadiq, by now clearly past his best, was also picked. Asif assumed the wickets in India would turn, so he brought two slow left-armers, a leg-spinner and just three seamers, and yet Kapil Dev and Ghavri took 47 of our wickets with seamers in the series on pitches that didn't always help the spinner. The first eleven players weren't pressurised by the reserves during the tour; we were picked on reputation and the selectors ignored our lack of depth. That became a criminal neglect when I ran into injury problems. I broke down in the second Test, was just a passenger in the next and missed the fourth when conditions would have been ideal for me. We were so short of seam bowlers that my injury disrupted us completely, yet it's a fair assumption that one of your opening bowlers will break down during a six Test series. That clearly hadn't occurred to the tour selectors and we paid the penalty.

The public interest in the tour was absolutely incredible. I had got used to hearing tales from Mushtaq and Intikhab about the Indian passion for cricket and we all yearned for the resumption of Tests between the two countries. Mushtaq's disappointment at missing the trip was obvious when he was interviewed on television and it made me realise how much this tour should mean to all of us. The scenes at the airport when we arrived in Delhi were remarkable; the whole country seemed to be on the verge of cricketing hysteria. Wherever we went, cricket was the sole subject of conversation. People who knew nothing about the game would still ask searching questions — what would I do on spinners' wickets and what internal politics had meant the exclusion of Sarfraz and Mushtaq? As for me, I felt marvellous. The absence of Sarfraz alerted me to the fact that I would have to do a lot of bowling, so I stepped up my training schedule. My action and run-up felt solidly integrated at last and I couldn't wait to thrive in the tremendous atmosphere of Tests in India.

The first Test was a draw, with both sides batting solidly. Although we were never in any real danger, the match was a bit of a jolt to our complacency. For a start, our opening pair looked vulnerable: Mudassar was all right but Majid, who had clearly said he didn't want to open, looked shaky. Our batting looked a little erratic and apart from Mudassar there were no grafters, nobody who could hang on in a crisis and grind the bowlers down. Our stroke makers might be dominant on the flat wickets in Pakistan, but they could prove unstable on surfaces that helped the bowlers. Above all, we were astonished at the incredible pressure exerted by a crowd jam-packed into a stadium. We had heard all about Indian crowds, but not until we had witnessed it did we realise how much they got behind their side. I hasten to add that they were always fair and quick to appreciate good play from us, but they were a great advantage to Indian morale. The Indian team had clearly improved in the past year and were younger and more enthusiastic in the field. Kapil Dev and Ghavri both seemed more confident players, Doshi had developed into a very tidy slow bowler, Vengsarkar's confidence had been boosted by some solid batting performances against England and Yashpal Sharma looked a talented, solid batsman. Under Gavaskar's leadership, India looked as if they knew where they were going.

We were lucky to escape with another draw in the second Test. By the time we arrived in Delhi half the team, including me, had gone down with a virus. I then pulled a muscle in my side and bowled only eight overs in the game. Just to pile on the agony, the wicket at Delhi was tailor-made for me: on the first morning it swung, seamed and bounced and remained lively throughout. Although drugged with pain killers to combat my virus, I still bowled six very quick overs on an ideal wicket for fast bowling. Then I was struck down with the side injury and it proved to be the worst injury I'd had up to that time in my career. I had to sit watching Sikander get us back in the game with a superb spell of bowling; he took eleven wickets in the match in marathon efforts. I felt the true misery of my injury in India's second innings, when they had to get 390 to win in a day and a half. The wicket was still helpful and the bounce uneven and I believe I would have assisted Sikander in winning the match. India were allowed to get off the hook and although we fought like tigers in the field we should have been beaten, but against our limited attack their batsmen didn't bat boldly enough and in the end, with wickets in hand, they finished twenty-six runs short. In the circumstances we were grateful that their ambitions had been so limited: Sikander was exhausted after his heroic efforts and our spin bowlers just did not make an impact. We lived to fight another day, but the series was turning out to be a complete contrast to the one of twelve months before.

I had just one week to get fit for the third Test. Dr Farrukh was the official team doctor and he diagnosed a muscle rupture; the only way to heal it was complete rest and heat treatment. The facilities in Delhi were excellent but Asif insisted that I accompany the team to Poona in accordance with his dictate that we should all remain together throughout the tour. Back in Bombay, I had two days practice before the start of the Test. I could feel some pain on the first day, but it was a little easier on the eve of the Test and I decided to take a chance and play. Unfortunately, we lost the toss and had to bowl first; another day's recuperation and I would have been almost completely recovered. The muscle went again in my first over as I put extra effort into a delivery; I couldn't leave the field in the first over of a Test match, so I bowled another fourteen in acute pain. I had a couple of pain-killing injections at lunchtime, but to no avail. By the last session, I was just running up and letting my arm go over: this was the time I was most needed, because India were 154 for 6 on a wicket helping the bowlers. Their tail-enders batted well and took them to 334, which proved to be a winning score. Having to sit helplessly watching the Indian tail get runs was a bitter experience for me — I was exhausted after my virus and some of my muscles that I didn't normally use were very painful as I had tried to bowl open-chested to relieve the agony in my side. I was feeling pretty sorry for myself, and felt that I'd let the side down. Yet our batsmen also let us down: the pitch was expected to aid their spinners, yet Roger Binny — a seamer — got the first three wickets as we played some extravagant strokes. Zaheer was exposed early in both innings and by now he was looking a shadow of his former self, and got out twice to strange shots. We simply failed to fight it out, even though India bowled well. In the end, we lost by 131 runs and the only people to blame were ourselves, though the umpiring decisions on the whole went against us.

I had to miss the drawn fourth Test because of my side injury. Once again the wicket would have been ideal for me — fifteen wickets fell on a grassy pitch in the first two days — and I was starting to believe that the luck which had blessed me in recent years was now turning the other way with a vengeance. The fact that I had been ruled out at such an important time in such a prestigious series was demoralising. It was almost a month before I felt properly fit to bowl flat out and then, on my first stint in the nets, I strained a back muscle! I just couldn't believe it; how could I explain this new injury after such a long rest? The press had for some reason continued to describe my side injury as a strained back muscle — well now they'd got what they wanted. I decided to keep quiet about the new injury and played the following day against East Zone to prove my fitness for the fifth Test. It got worse and a couple of times I almost had to go off the field. Luckily I only had to bowl a few overs in the match against weak batting so my colleagues weren't too worried about my bowling within myself. When we got to Madras for the Test, I was hoping that the back strain would gradually ease but every time I put some effort into my bowling in the nets, the pain returned. I was worried sick. I felt I hadn't pulled my weight on the tour and dared not tell Asif that I had picked up a fresh injury while resting an old one. I secretly consulted the best specialist I could find, and he advised me to miss the Madras Test. I said that was impossible, so he advised ionization treatment during every interval. That relieved the pain for a time but it kept returning. I just gritted my teeth and carried on with the pain always there. Five over spells were all I could manage on my first day of bowling and with Gavaskar batting impeccably on a perfect wicket, I was very down. However, I bowled better the next day with the pain not so intense: I picked up my hundredth Test wicket when bowling Kirmani and finished with 5 for 114, a pleasing performance in the circumstances. At last I was achieving something in this series. Without Gavaskar's 166, India would have struggled, but he was in his most impregnable form, he never took a chance against me, and waited till I had finished my spells before taking the other bowlers apart in cool, efficient style.

If only our batsmen had taken a leaf from Gavaskar's book! In the second innings, they gave the worst exhibition I've ever seen from a Pakistan side. We were dismissed for 272 in six hours on an ideal batting wicket. At one time, we were 58 for 5, batting with incredible indiscipline; within an hour of finishing my thirty-eight-over bowling stint, I was padding up. Not one wicket fell to good bowling. Javed and Wasim Raja both got fifties, but they thrashed around as if they had a train to catch. Doshi bowled a tight line and length and Kapil kept attacking, but we just gave it to them. By this time, Zaheer was completely shattered, and convinced he'd never get a run in India. He was sure someone had put an evil spell on him: at the end of the tour he received a telegram saying: 'I've lifted the black magic on you at last, now you will get runs again.' Zaheer believed all that stuff.

Our morale after Madras was the lowest I could recall in my Test career. We had just lost a Test by ten wickets when we should have had no trouble at all in playing for a draw. We salvaged some self-respect in the final Test but, typical of a demoralised team, we dropped four catches and the game petered out into a draw. I took nine wickets altogether and at last I was fully fit and bowled my best of the tour. By a savage irony the series was ending just as I was getting to grips with the Indian batsmen. That seemed to sum up my fortunes in 1979.

At the end of the tour, we were a very demoralised bunch and dreading a hostile reception back home. Defeat by India had seemed unthinkable a few months earlier and Asif, no doubt fearing the worst, announced his retirement from Test cricket before we got home. We knew that a sustained whispering campaign against us had been going on in the press for most of the tour (we were supposed to be wining and dining women and indulging in debauchery), and I was singled out for particularly ill-informed gossip. Apparently I had pulled my back muscle through my lecherous activities with actresses, and I wasn't training at all. No one seemed to notice that this was the first time I had missed several important matches since my Test debut in 1971; no other fast bowler of Test class had enjoyed such a good run. The journalists who concocted these fantastic stories about our alleged womanising obviously saw us being mobbed wherever we went and decided that we had had taken advantage of such enthusiasm. That would have been impossible because we were locked up in our hotel room at 10.30 every night — without female company. Never had I been on a tour of so many petty rules and regulations. The management were so worried about press distortions that they shackled us right from the start of the tour. I disagreed with such a regimented atmosphere because we needed some sort of relaxation amid the fantastic tension of that Indian series. It was painful to turn down so many party invitations, but as they all started after ten o'clock, we had no option. We couldn't unwind at all and never really got away from the cricket. As a result, the ridiculous stories in some sections of the press were doubly infuriating.

I have never experienced in one series such pressure coming from so many quarters — the amazing crowds, our poor form, the knowledge that the Pakistan public would be very angry at our efforts, my injury problem and the narrow-minded social restrictions. It was easy to lose sight amid all the traumas that we were only playing a game of cricket. As usual after a Pakistan defeat, a reshuffle was deemed essential. The Chairman of our Board of Control resigned and his successor started to consider candidates for the captaincy after Asif's resignation. Our arrival time at Lahore Airport was kept a secret in case we were given some rough treatment and the customs officials, those reliable barometers of public opinion, left us in no doubt of our fall from grace by delaying us for an hour, and even confiscating some magazines. When we've returned from a good tour, they usually wave us through! Such is the price we pay for representing a country that takes defeat as a national disaster. To lose to India was clearly the most heinous crime imaginable.

I can smile at such over-reaction now, but at the time, I felt very unhappy. I felt deeply the shame of our poor performances in 1979 and the Indian debacle was the worst of all. In just one year, our international reputation had slumped. We were now a second-rate cricketing team, with some of our best players apparently on the way out. No real successors to Majid, Sadiq, Asif, Mushtaq and (possibly) Zaheer were coming through, a situation caused by the haphazard state of our own domestic cricket. The established players had not been put under enough pressure to come up with Test-class performances. A tougher approach was absolutely necessary in the future.

In all honesty, I could not reproach myself for a feeling of over-confidence during that dreadful year. I was too busy trying to improve my bowling and attempting to curtail the rashness in my batting — sometimes with gratifying success, often with some annoying lapses from grace. Yet I never failed to give everything to the side and indeed my back strain on the Indian tour had stemmed from over-enthusiasm in trying to bowl too fast too soon after injury. I knew that I had to train even harder and develop further my all-round abilities as quickly as possible to help get us out of our rut.

9 The Path to the Captaincy

From 1980 to 1982, I played in four series for Pakistan that continued to reveal our limitations. We beat Australia at home because the wickets were prepared in our favour; the West Indies beat us through superior fast bowling, inflicting our first home defeat since 1969; we lost an acrimonious series in Australia through bad batting and team selection; and we outplayed Sri Lanka, even with a weakened side. I was unaware of it at the time, but a chain of events had started that propelled me into the captaincy of my country.

Throughout this period of erratic performances by Pakistan, I managed to maintain my form. I scored my first Test hundred — against the West Indies on my twenty-eighth birthday after coming in at 95 for 5 — and in the same series became the second Pakistani to reach the Test 'double' of 1,000 runs and 100 wickets. During the series in Australia, I became the top Pakistani wicket-taker in Tests and against Sri Lanka, I took 14 wickets in a match, the best return by a bowler in Tests in Pakistan. My county form for Sussex was satisfactory, once I'd sorted out whether or not I was going to play regularly for them. At the start of the 1980 season, my worst fears were confirmed when they gave me a one-year contract and told me that I would be playing in the one-day games, while Wessels and le Roux would be the first-choice overseas couple for the county games. I protested that bowlers win matches, not solid, high-scoring batsmen but Arnold Long, our captain, was too safety-conscious about batting. When Wessels was injured, I managed to prove the point. Le Roux and I formed a very successful opening pair on the fast Hove wicket and we ended up the first two in the bowling averages for Sussex, lifting the team to fourth in the table after a disastrous start. At the end of the season, Wessels left to live in Australia, so my place was secure. In 1981, le Roux and I were again in fine form with bat and ball and we finished second in the championship table, missing the title by just two points. A change of captaincy, John Barclay for Arnold Long, had worked wonders and I was happy with life at Hove once more.

I was not all that happy with the appointment of Javed Miandad as Pakistan's captain after our disastrous tour of India. Majid seemed the obvious choice, but as he had played poorly in India, he was ruled out of contention. Although Javed won his first series — against Australia — it was an undemanding test of his skills. We won the first Test on a turning wicket, and the other two Tests were played on dead wickets that gave no hope of a positive result. From the first day, everyone knew there was nothing but boring, purposeless cricket ahead, no wonder Dennis Lillee told me he wouldn't be coming back to Pakistan! This ridiculous bias in favour of batsmen did us no favours at all. Huge totals by our batsmen simply papered over the cracks and brought no tension into the game; when we needed to play at our best in crises during subsequent series, we were unfitted for the task.

Our next series showed how much we still had to learn. The West Indies came to Pakistan, and in winning 1–0 they looked the better team. The slow pitches didn't deter their pacemen from getting wickets; the Test we lost was a spinner's wicket yet their quick bowlers got fifteen wickets on it. We lacked a reliable opening pair, our middle-order batting was brittle, we had no team spirit. Croft, Marshall and Clarke bowled very effectively for the West Indies and Garner was an excellent stock bowler.

Viv Richards regularly showed his class when he was really needed by his side and in contrast Zaheer had another miserable time, averaging 14. He was hit on the head by Clarke and I must admit that I thought Zaheer was finished at that stage; he did very well to fight back a year later. Mudassar, another batsman who became an integral part of the side, was treated poorly in this West Indies Series. He was dropped after failing in a one-day International, even though his style of batting was suited for Tests.

The 1981–82 tour to Australia magnified our decline. On paper a 2–1 defeat was adequate, yet our solitary victory was on a slow, low Melbourne wicket reminiscent of conditions back home. The toss was crucial, a big score gave us a psychological cushion and our spinners bowled well. At Perth and Brisbane we were bowled out in a lamentable fashion, showing little resolution. Our bowlers did excellently in the first Test to dismiss Australia for 180 on a good Perth wicket but I shall never forget our batting collapse that day. Our first wicket fell as I was taking off one of my boots; our second went as the other one was pulled off and four wickets were down by the time I'd taken off my damp clothes. My batting boots were swiftly found and I walked out with the score 21 for 5 — soon it was 26 for 8 and if it hadn't been for some good hitting by Sarfraz, we would never have got anywhere near our eventual total of 62. In our second innings we showed little fight and lost easily by 286 runs. Lillee, as expected, had bowled superbly in the first innings but the way we capitulated to the off-spin of Yardley in the second innings showed that we were very dispirited.

We were always up against it thereafter and morale began to collapse like a pack of cards. We lost the next Test by ten wickets in the most ignominious fashion. In the first innings, almost everyone got established, yet only Zaheer got over fifty in a total of 291. Greg Chappell showed us how to bat making 201 in calm, sensible style on a bland wicket. All we had to do was bat out the last day to draw and Mudassar and Mohsin Khan gave us the right platform with an opening stand of 72. In just four hours, we were bowled out for 223. Only Mudassar (out to a nasty bouncer from Lillee) wasn't at fault as we all threw our wickets away. It was a pathetic batting effort. The subsequent face-saving victory at Melbourne was explained by the fact that Australia picked an attack which relied too much on fast bowling, and because we managed to capitalise on the conditions. It was significant that our captain, Javed, agreed with his opposite number Greg Chappell that the pitch should be dug up and indeed the Australian Board threatened to play the forthcoming Test against England elsewhere unless something drastic was attempted to make the contest fairer. So none of us read too much into our victory.

We returned to Pakistan and faced the inevitable barrage of criticism for our Australian displays. The press said we were a second-class cricketing nation and in truth, that was difficult to counter. Hardly any of our batsmen had played with responsibility — fifties weren't being turned into hundreds anymore. The tour party had been badly selected: it was known that two of the three Test grounds had bounce, yet we didn't bring a leg-spinner like Abdul Qadir. We chose a youngster, Rizwan-us-Zaman, who had plenty of promise, but was still very raw. He was picked to open in the first Test and made 0 and 8. I felt sorry for him; he was short of experience at home and yet he was now expected to open against Lillee and Alderman on unfamiliar fast, bouncy wickets. Everyone had known before the tour started that we needed to find a number three batsman — Zaheer had put his request to go down the order in writing to the Board. Yet no notice was taken. It was like a nightmare come true: when the inevitable crisis came, Mansoor and Majid were thrown in at the deep end. We had to fly out Mohsin Khan as a replacement when he should have been on the tour in the first place. He looked streets ahead of anyone in playing fast bowling, with his great natural ability and it was so sad that he had taken so long to blossom.

The two people responsible for the selections were Javed and the manager, Ijaz Butt. Throughout the tour, Javed had been complaining that he hadn't been given the team he wanted, but then why did he accept it? When we returned to Pakistan after the Australian trip the whole team was rather surprised that Javed had kept the job. Then the Board issued a statement that really started something — it said that we failed in Australia because the senior players hadn't co-operated with the captain. All of us were furious at such a slur: we could not accept this public statement. No sportsman likes to be accused of deliberately letting down his country. To us it was clear that the statement summarised Javed's views. Of course there were personality clashes with the captain because there had been communication problems with some of the players. Sadly the captaincy didn't suit Javed because previously he was always so full of fun and he seemed to try to change his personality and his attitude to the team which wasn't always successful. His man management was poor and even though he tried his best on the field, the team just didn't click under his leadership. Too many senior players were much older than him and he lacked the strength of character to drag the team along under his wing. That had been obvious since his first series as captain two years earlier, yet here he was sanctioning a statement from the Board that alleged deliberate failure to co-operate with him.

I blame the Board more than Javed; they should have taken note of Javed's views, then put them to the senior players and refrained from public remarks until the matter was settled either way. The unsavoury allegations delighted the press and inflamed the public for a time. The integrity of the players had been questioned, talk of conspiracies was in the air, yet at no stage on the

Australian tour had any of us gathered to talk about Javed's captaincy. We eventually did meet to discuss the Board's statement: everyone was so upset by the mishandling of the situation and Javed's part in it that we took a decision we knew might be misinterpreted. Ten of us issued our own statement which questioned Javed's ability to lead the side and spelled out our refusal to play under his captaincy. Majid was appointed our spokesman, the press drummed up the old cliche of Lahore cricketers being hostile to their counterparts from Karachi, and the Board refused to back down. As a result, eight of us missed the first two Tests against Sri Lanka — Majid, Mohsin, Mudassar, Sarfraz, Sikander, Wasim Bari, Zaheer and me.

By now the country was in a ferment. The tour to England was only a couple of months away and the tour party had to be named soon. Who would captain the party? Would the senior players be on the trip? Would it be another poor showing in England from a Pakistan side weakened by the unavailability of star players? Memories were still very fresh of our abject performance in England in 1978 and clearly the public pressure was getting to the Board, especially after our second team almost lost the Faisalabad Test to Sri Lanka. With the Lahore Test imminent and the threat of crowd disturbances very real, a compromise was reached — Javed would be captain in the final Test but would announce his unavailability for the captaincy on the England tour. He would, however, be available as a player. The senior players came back at Lahore, we won by an innings and although our initial dealings with Javed were strained, they mellowed with the passage of time.

The whole affair had been appallingly handled. I believe we had no option but to make our stand once the issue had become public property. Again it underlined how important a bad defeat is to the Pakistan cricket-lover. Some other countries take a more sensible view of such reverses, accepting that the other side had better cricketers or more luck. In Pakistan however, because of some sensational and emotional journalism, it has to be a case of politics (i.e. Lahore v Karachi), womanizing or personality clashes among the players, never cricketing defects.

With Javed removed from the captaincy, the choice of his successor again divided the nation. Gradually I began to emerge as a compromise candidate; Javed wouldn't play under Zaheer, Majid's form was doubtful and there were no obvious contenders. I had been one of the eight to stand out against Javed, but there were no other rivals from the ranks of those who sided with the Board, Wasim Raja was the only possibility, but he might not keep his place in the team. I was therefore offered the job.

Only two people had previously thought that I might have been captaincy material. One was Sarfraz after the Australian tour ended and the other was one of my cousins two years earlier. Dr Farrukh Ahmad Khan had been the team doctor on our trip to India in 1979 to 80 and during my spells of treatment, he got to know my views on what was going wrong. At the end of that tour he startled me by saying I should be the next captain. I was flattered at his remarks, but thought no more about them until the Board offered me the job in 1982.

It took me a day or two before I decided to accept. Some close friends like Iftikhar Ahmad, the country's top TV cricket commentator, advised me against it, citing Ian Botham's decline after being made captain as a warning. Yet captaincy is after all about temperament, and I reasoned that an all-rounder had a better chance of understanding what made both his batsmen and bowlers tick. I hadn't forgotten how little Mushtaq seemed to know about dealings with fast bowlers. I hadn't captained a side since Oxford in 1974 but I had never been one to switch off while fielding at fine leg, waiting for my next bowling stint. I had always tried to think about the game once I'd got established in the Test team and the captaincy would be a stimulating mental challenge. Intikhab, my former captain, was to be the tour manager and I was confident he would be a great help. As a great admirer of the captaincy of Ian Chappell and the way he led by example with guts and pride, I would try to approach that kind of leadership.

In the end I accepted because I wasn't ambitious for the captaincy. Of course, I felt honoured but I knew that I wouldn't be side-tracked by the need to save face, the obsession of some captains to avoid defeat at all costs. I thought to myself, 'It's no big deal if I fail — I shall give it back if I can't do it. It's far more important to keep playing for Pakistan.' I believed sincerely that things couldn't be as bad under my leadership as they were in Australia. I knew that at times I would be wrapped up in my bowling and that I might miss something on the field; I was determined to be open with the players and expect them to point out things to me. One of my pet hates in cricket has always been captains who were too inflexible in their tactics, who reacted tetchily to any constructive suggestions from colleagues: some captains of my experience feel that if anyone advises them it's an insult and go to great pains to show who the boss is!

I knew I would be blamed if we played badly, so I insisted on having the decisive say in the selection of the tour party. I wasn't going to fall into the same trap Javed fell in in Australia of moaning about the make-up of the squad and hinting that the captain's wishes had been overruled by the selectors. If we failed, I would take the responsibility square on my shoulders. In the end I got my own way and the result was the most rewarding tour of my career.

10   The England Tour

I really enjoyed my first tour as captain. The fact that it was in England was doubly satisfying: my memories of my abysmal efforts in 1971 were still fresh. Before the tour everyone was expecting me to fail, but at the end, Pakistan's reputation stood high and that was important to me, after our poor performances in recent series. The off-field pressures didn't bother me — the English cricket media was far more civilised than some sections in Pakistan who were waiting for me to fail, especially in Karachi. I was lucky to have such a great manager in Intikhab. He looked after everything behind the scenes, making sure that all the party arrived in the right place at the right time, and so on, baggage intact. Having been sceptical about the role of a manager in county cricket, I can now state with complete conviction that he is invaluable to a Test captain. I thought team spirit was good: we proved that in subsequent series against Australia and India. The Tests were exciting affairs and with a little more luck and appropriate application from our batmen, I feel that our 2–1 deficit could easily have been turned into a 3–0 advantage. On the one occasion that our batting really clicked (at Lord's) we won by ten wickets and we did after all take more wickets than England in the series. In the end, we were let down by temperament.

I was happy with the selection of the party. I got my own way over everyone and only had to fight hard for the leg-spinner Abdul Qadir. It was argued that he hadn't done much on the 1978 tour of England, but as a big wicket-taker in Pakistan cricket in the previous winter, he was more confident and experienced; but the main reason was that Test batsmen hadn't seen top-class bowling from a leg-spinner for years. His selection was justified as none of the England batsmen had a clue how to play him and he was devastating against the county sides. Initially, I had some problem in captaining him; I didn't really know how to set a field for spinners, so I let him get on with it. Eventually I imposed my will more, especially when I thought he was bowling defensively. I'd tell him that he was in the team to attack batsmen, that they were baffled by him; he needed to be told he was bowling well. Much was made of the fact that his bowling average was high, without people realising that he was attacking, yet keeping an end sealed up at the same time. The Test wickets were all too slow for him, so that on the many occasions he beat the bat, the edge wouldn't carry to the close fielders. Yet at Lord's he opened up the game for us, by getting four wickets in the first innings, helping us make them follow on. He bowled a lot of overs, so his average would inevitably suffer, but I thought he had a great influence on our out-cricket.

Team selection wasn't really a problem on the tour: I told everyone that players would be selected on merit for the Tests, not reputation. I had seen too much complacency among our players on other tours and it wasn't going to happen this time. We cruised through our county matches leading up to the Tests, but I wasn't taken in by that — the counties were resting their best bowlers and our batsmen were picking up cheap runs. No one had to bat in a crisis until the first Test, and that's where we came unstuck.

The first Test was in our hands on three occasions, but we let it slip. I felt the tension greatly: it was my debut as captain and because of a thigh injury, I was a doubtful starter right up to the last minute. We did marvellously to bowl them out cheaply on an easy-paced Edgbaston wicket on the first day, but then we batted badly in ideal sunny conditions the following day; many of us got twenties and thirties, but no one got in for very long to grind out a big score. My first innings effort with the bat proved to be a watershed in my career — I got out to a dreadful shot and so I couldn't reprimand the other batsmen about their rashness. I then decided I wouldn't throw my wicket away again and I fought it out for the rest of the series, batting responsibly.

If our batting in the first innings was frustrating so was our ill-fortune the following day. England had led by just 21 and we soon had them 146 for 6 in their second innings. Derek Randall got a hundred and although I admired his unconventional methods, he was still very fortunate against Qadir; he also should have been caught early on in the slips off my bowling, but Zaheer didn't see the ball. We reduced them to 212 for 9 and the game was there for the taking. Unfortunately my leg injury that had bothered me for a week became aggravated, Tahir Naqqash was fatigued after a great stint and Sikander looked short of penetration and confidence. Tahir's spectacular spell had been magnificent and so timely: I had been struggling on pain-killers and I was almost out of the match as a bowler when he dragged us back in contention with a great spell after lunch. Eventually he tired and our attack again looked short of a cutting edge. As a result Bob Willis and Bob Taylor added a vital 79 for the last wicket against an attack that was on its knees after getting early breakthroughs. The critics, of course, were insistent that I should have taken the new ball once the stand became entrenched, but they weren't to know about my injury, nor the depth of Tahir's fatigue; for his part, Abdul Qadir was bowling superbly, beating the bat twice an over and looking likely to get a wicket at any time.

Despite such frustration, we could still have won the

game on the fourth day, when we needed 313 for victory, with two days ahead of us. With our strong batting line-up, that was within our capabilities, but at 98 for 7, my optimism was mocking me. Ian Botham dismissed Mudassar for his second nought of the match, which forced me to have words with him afterwards. Mudassar seemed totally overawed by the physical presence and aggression of the English bowlers.

Whatever the reasons for his lack of success, Mudassar had left our top order exposed — he came into the Test with an average of 291 and we badly needed his grit and solidity to get us off on the right foot. Instead of this our batsmen came in and started playing shots right away, which may have been entertaining for the crowd but infuriated me. The occasion got to us; those easy runs against undemanding county bowlers had done little for our preparation for the crunch games. I was pleased to be able to play the right sort of innings in the circumstances, making 65 and, with the help of the tail-enders, managing to put a gloss of respectability on our efforts. It wasn't good enough however and defeat by 113 runs was a bitter blow, considering how many chances we'd had to win that Test.

My mind was not solely on the result at the end of the game, however. Our own defects had annoyed me and I would make sure we improved in application and concentration. That was in our own hands but what wasn't within our control was the standard of umpiring. I was very disturbed at some of the decisions of umpires Evans and Palmer. Mike Gatting was given the benefit of the doubt for an lbw appeal off my bowling that was the plumbest lbw I've seen for a long time, while Mohsin was given out lbw to Botham in the second innings in debatable circumstances. Even more astonishing was the lbw decision that went against Mudassar on the first day — it was ridiculously high. After the game, umpire Palmer accused us of appealing a lot. He said that if all our appeals had been given, then England would have scored hardly a run; I presume he was referring specifically to Abdul Qadir and his many appeals for lbw or catches in the bat/pad position. What Palmer didn't take into account was the fact that we had a leg-spinner who could bowl the googly, operating with two men in the bat/pad position, against batsmen who didn't have a clue which way the ball was turning. Clearly the umpires didn't know which way the ball was spinning, either. On a slow, low wicket, we were bound to appeal more, with so many men around the bat. Most of the shouts from us were very close indeed and there were no orchestrated appeals. When you see English batsmen padding away the googly, you're bound to appeal! As far as I was concerned, Edgbaston was a high-pressure match; a good umpire, like a good batsman, thrives under such tension.

All of us involved in Tests have to live with pressure. That point was made clear to Javed Miandad after his first innings attempt to knock Hemmings out of the firing line which backfired on the batsmen. From the first morning, I'd had a close-up glimpse of how the pressure was affecting my opposite number, Bob Willis. As we tossed the coin, he was white, very tense, and unable to say much; he had already led England in three Tests and was far more experienced than me, yet it was getting to him. In my first game as a Test captain, I was fully aware that many were expecting, and others were waiting, for me to fail. That first day at Edgbaston was incredibly tense for me and in the circumstances, my return of 7 for 58 gave me immense satisfaction.

Before the Lord's Test, we had to wait until the very latest for my injury to heal and when we got it all together to win, the pleasure was massive. Although the ten-wicket margin was comfortable, we were fighting against the weather for most of the time. We also had two bowlers injured in England's second innings, but Mudassar more than filled the gap with his underrated medium pace swingers. Stubborn partnerships held us up on the last day when we were desperate to get back into the series before the rain washed play out. A solid team effort got us through and I was very proud. Mohsin's 200 was the rock on which our big total was built and although he deservedly received great praise, he was a little impetuous in places. He played and missed a lot and the England bowlers made it easier for him by bowling the wrong line — he loves to drive and relished the many deliveries pitched up, on, or outside, his off-stump. Later in his innings, they got it right, blocking the on-side and bowling straight at him. I thought the tactics by David Gower, standing in as captain for the injured Willis, were a little strange; he had an unbalanced attack and he bowled Botham too long and Ian Greig not enough. They looked rather disjointed in the field. Having said all that, I don't want to take anything away from Mohsin because it was a delight to see one of our batsmen stay at the crease long enough to score a double hundred — but later in the year, he played even better against Australia and India. That Lord's knock clearly gave him the confidence to make his mark in Test cricket and he went on to play a succession of classy innings.

With rain disrupting so much of the play, it soon became clear that we had to make England follow-on if we were to win. As a result, their first innings was a very intense affair, with Qadir's leg-spin preying on the batsmen's nerves. The tension led to another brush with an umpire that tarnished Pakistan's image, even though our many critics failed to put the incident within the context of a terribly tense part of the game. Ian Botham was batting along with Gower as we attacked, trying desperately for the breakthrough that would give us a chance of forcing the follow-on; Qadir appealed for lbw against Botham and umpire Constant turned the appeal down. Qadir was heavily criticised for his attitude to Constant's decision; all I can say is that it's easy for the press box pundits to make such sweeping statements, but they really don't know the frustration that all of us felt at the decision. Of course, I appreciate that we weren't the first side to feel the tension at a vital stage in a Test when we were one down in the series, with the weather threatening to ruin our chances. Very few seemed to understand the frustration that Qadir must have felt during a particularly engrossing period of play when he had bowled beautifully at Gower and Botham. In the best traditions of leg-spin bowling, he had spun a web round the batsmen and was starting to trap them. Botham played for a leg-break and Qadir bowled him a 'flipper' that went straight on at speed; he played all round it and it would have hit middle and leg. He was absolutely plumb; I thought so at the time and television action replays subsequently confirmed this. Qadir's frustration stemmed from the fact that on this occasion umpire Constant couldn't tell the difference between a leg-break and the ball that goes straight on. It was beginning to dawn on me that umpiring decisions might play a distressingly crucial part in this series; Lord's again proved that the pressure was getting to some of them. It was to become a subject to be debated at great length at the end of the series.

Luckily for us, Mudassar helped distract us from our sense of grievance by a match-winning spell of bowling, after we had just managed to force the follow-on. We were also lucky that Mike Gatting accepted the offer of bad light from the umpires and decided to go off on the Saturday night. Gatting and Jackman, the last wicket pair, only needed a couple of runs to avoid the follow-on and we were exhausted after being in the field all day. Gatting only needed to get a couple of runs and the game was dead. The following morning, amid great tension, I managed to get Jackman with an inswinging yorker and Gatting was left stranded. Mudassar then did the rest. To the great amazement of many, he took 6 for 32 with deliveries that swung alarmingly late; at one stage we had England 9 for 3. My decision to bowl Mudassar certainly didn't stem from imaginative captaincy: with Sarfraz and Tahir injured, we had little choice. He has always been a good shiner of the ball — as most Pakistanis are, simply because the ball doesn't seam back home and you have to work hard at preserving the shine of hard surfaces — and he managed to get it all right on the day. In the previous Test, his four overs had looked very ordinary but he is better than he looks. He has a high action and strong wrist movement and the fact that he bowls wide of the crease can make him a disconcerting proposition as the ball swings in very late. Mudassar is a self-effacing character who doesn't rate his bowling all that highly, yet in the nets he'll invariably bowl one of our best batsmen with an absolute beauty. At Lord's, he did a marvellous job but it wasn't the first time he had picked up valuable wickets in Tests. Many batsmen had paid the penalty for under-rating him.

With England up against it, the rest of the match concerned the equation between time and wickets. Chris Tavare and Ian Botham batted very responsibly in their second innings and the occasional shower of rain increased our frustration. I was criticised for delaying the taking of the second new ball, but the old one was still swinging and Mudassar didn't know how to use the new ball properly. If Tahir or Sarfraz had been available it would have been different; a new ball is invaluable when it's in the hands of bowlers who can use it to their advantage, otherwise it can easily accelerate the scoring rate. Anyway we had to take it in the end and after one over from Mudassar, Qadir eased my worries by getting rid of the obdurate Jackman and we were left to get 76 from eighteen overs. I sent in Javed along with Mohsin because I thought his speed between the wickets and wide array of strokes would be decisive. It worked and despite a defensive field, we got there with four overs to

spare. Pakistan had waited a long time for this victory —
only our second in Tests in England, and at Lord's as well.
For once, we had made our superiority count. We had
done ourselves justice and in the process set up the series
for a tremendous finish. That Lord's Test was one of the
great moments of my cricketing life, considering our
distractions of injuries and uncertain weather. Despite
my injury, I bowled my best of the series, beating the bat
countless times. On the final day, I bowled 29 consecutive
overs, keeping it going by sheer willpower after spending
three days in succession in the field.

The third Test was a remarkably tense game, in the very
best traditions of Test cricket. Unfortunately, our batsmen
lost us the match and we were unlucky with injuries. We
couldn't play either Sarfraz or Tahir and had to call up
Ehtesham-ud-Din, an experienced seamer who had
played four times for Pakistan. He was playing at the time
in the Bolton Association League and as a result was not
properly fit for a five-day Test. He pulled a muscle and
couldn't bowl in the second innings when he would have
been very useful on a pitch that favoured a seamer like
him. If Sarfraz had been fully fit, his bowling and indeed
his stubborn batting would have been absolutely invaluable.

Throughout, the pitch was slow and gave help to the
bowlers, but that cannot excuse our lack of batting
application. Mohsin played a ridiculous shot, driving at
the first ball of our second innings, Zaheer chased a wide
one in his desire to dominate right from the start, and
Javed got himself out ten minutes before lunch, having
put us back in the match in the second innings with a fast
fifty. Eventually Abdul Qadir batted sensibly to help me
add 42 runs, then Sikander stayed while we put on a
further thirty. At 199 for 8, a lead of 218, we were dealt a
savage blow by the umpire. Vic Marks came on to bowl
off-breaks and his second over was punctuated by two
ridiculous appeals for either catches at short leg or lbw —

I wasn't sure what the bowler and close fielders were imagining in their appeals. The third appeal in that over seemed equally ridiculous when the umpire gave Sikander out, caught by Gatting at short-leg. I was absolutely dumbfounded; his bat was well away from the ball on impact, it was hidden behind his pad in approved defensive fashion. It was ridiculous appealing — the same offence we had been accused of by the press during the series and it went a long way towards costing us the match. Now I know I stand accused of over-reaction, but consider the facts — we were 218 ahead on a pitch that would not get any easier. The fallibility of the England batting was well known and there was no guarantee that they would get over two hundred in such conditions. They were rattled during my partnership with Sikander because he was batting very sensibly. England had just four regular bowlers in their side because of their need to bolster the batting and by the time Sikander and I had got established, they were all very tired. Willis had to turn to Marks in desperation on a pitch showing no signs of taking spin. Another thirty runs from our partnership and who knows?

We fought magnificently when England batted in search of 219 for victory. When they were 172 for 3 it looked all over against our weakened attack, but we fielded superbly and Mudassar again showed his worth, taking four more wickets. They ended the day on 189 for 6, still thirty runs adrift and in some panic; Botham was the danger man and we thought that if we got him early on the last morning, we would win. We got the wicket we wanted off the eleventh ball the next day and with Marks and Taylor at the wicket, the match was delicately poised. I rather let the team down at the crucial stage with some wayward bowling; it had rained in the night and the footholds were still a little damp, which caused me some problems when I was trying to land on solid ground just before delivery. We didn't have enough runs in hand to

Imran with Wasim Bari who in 1976 was the best wicket-keeper in the world.

Hitting a six off Eddie Hemmings during his second innings score of 65 in the Edgbaston Test 1982.

England *v* Pakistan, first Test at Edgbaston 1982. Although England won, Imran was named Man of the Match but was disappointed at losing his first Test as captain.

The 1982 series was won by England 2–1. The two captains are seen here being interviewed by Peter West.

The captain and his team; the Pakistan team that toured England 1982.

Leeds 1982; hooking
Ian Botham to the
boundary.

The vital wicket at Lord's in
the second Test, 1982, when
Imran dismissed Jackman
and enforced the follow-on.

The effort that goes into fast bowling can be seen in this sequence taken during the 1982 test at Edgbaston.

Imran takes himself off during his 7 wickets for 52 at Edgbaston 1982 to have a welcome drink, Abdul Qadir looks on.

January 1983 and the end of the duel with Kapil Dev

Imran meeting the President of Pakistan, at the dinner the President gave in the winter of 1982.

The classical action of Imran.

allow me to change ends and my erratic bowling gave Wasim Bari, our wicket-keeper, some worries. I felt fresh and fully in control of my nerves, but when my team really needed a controlled, accurate burst from me, it didn't come. All credit to Marks and Taylor for batting coolly to see England home by three wickets, but I felt disappointed with my efforts on that final morning.

That sense of anti-climax was still there when I made my remarks about the umpiring in the press conference after the match. I must add that I would have said the same, whether we had won or lost. Having played enough Test cricket for more than a decade, I feel I can take a beating, and although it was easy to construe my comments as sour grapes, that was not the case. I was asked direct questions about the umpiring standards and as it is in my nature to speak frankly, I did so. I complained about the Sikander dismissal and also added the decision that went against us in the first innings, when Gower got a big nick to Wasim Bari off Qadir's bowling but was reprieved. He hadn't reached double figures at the time, but went on to make 74, the second highest total of a low-scoring match. It was no use people telling me that these things even themselves out — they don't in a tight Test Match, as the decisions over Sikander and Gower proved, so what was all this about the law of averages? One decision in a tight situation can alter the balance of a series when the sides are as evenly matched as they were in the 1982 series. It was said that we appealed too often but we never complained about Jackman's loud, regular appeals when he was bowling, we accepted that he was trying his best for his country and was pretty keyed-up. All three Tests were played on slow wickets with low bounce, which inevitably meant there would be many close things as the ball kept low. If you add a leg-spinner who also bowls googlies, and my line of bowling which features a great deal of inswing plus the late inswing of Mudassar, it was clear there would be times when the pads would be rapped in very close situations. If we had nothing but bowlers who sent the ball away from the bat, there would obviously be fewer appeals because the issues would be more straightforward; the same applies if the wickets had been bouncy. At Hove there are always less appeals because the wicket has bounce and the ball often goes over the top of the stumps, while it's very different in Pakistan, the West Indies or the Test grounds in England. The umpires' attitude eventually got to us in the England series and it meant we missed one wicket by not appealing. It happened at Lord's when Ian Greig, my county teammate, told me that one of England's best batsmen was palpably out, caught at short-leg off Qadir, but nobody appealed!

I wish all umpires approached the standard of 'Dickie' Bird, who is the best I've ever known because he's consistent; he's known to be a 'not outer' among umpires and that's fair enough, because he remains that way. I also rate Barry Meyer, but I wasn't satisfied with the rest in the England series. I had been calling for neutral umpires for Tests since the Indian series in 1978, when the decisions went our way; my experiences in New Zealand in 1979 and then later in the year only confirmed my opinion that it was time to pool our umpiring resources and select a panel that would be the best in the world. I had made a point of commending the umpires on my Australian tour in 1976, so it wasn't just a case of my being negative and knocking. I was always ready to give praise to the umpires when it was deserved, because it is a demanding task with the growth of television coverage and the increase in slow, low wickets. I believe that the home side is subconsciously favoured by the umpires. There will always be tight situations in Tests but in my experience the home side gets the benefit of the doubt on more occasions than not. Neutral umpires, backed up by electronic aids, would help in that direction. It would be a move towards professionalism and if gadgets could help make the umpires' job easier, why not try them? Men like 'Dickie' Bird, Barry Meyer, Tom Brooks (Australia), and Douglas Sang Hue (West Indies) have been excellent umpires in my experience and if they umpired in a series in Pakistan, then flew over to Australia, I believe their influence and integrity would inspire others. In Pakistan, the umpiring is on the upgrade — Mahboob Shah and Shakoor Rana have come over to England to stand in county seasons and the experience has been invaluable. They have brought home fresh ideas about umpiring and the improvement has been so noticeable that both Kim Hughes and Sunil Gavaskar were at great pains not to blame the umpires after we had beaten Australia and India at home recently — an unprecedented occurrence in Pakistan.

I suppose it was easy to misinterpret my views about the umpiring standards in the immediate afermath of losing a match at Leeds. They should be able to accept criticism as we players have to; they're not sacred and they make human errors like we all do. Anyone who had ever interviewed me at length in the recent past knew that I had often called for a solution to something that's been a recurring problem in world cricket. One final word on the umpiring controversy — and it illustrates the double standards that are rife at the moment. When England returned from their unsuccessful tour to Australia, there was much comment about the umpires. Bob Willis said nothing about it, that was his choice and I respect him for being consistent. Yet George Mann, the chairman of the Test and County Cricket Board was widely quoted as saying that the team had kept its composure in the face of some bad umpiring decisions in Australia. He was right, but if it's fair enough for the head of the most important cricket body in England to pass public judgement on the Australian umpires, then why was it so unsporting for the Pakistan captain to make a similar judgement on the

English umpires just six months previously? Either captains, managers or top administrators are allowed to pass public comment, or they are not — at the moment it's permissible for an Englishman, but not for a Pakistani.

Apart from the umpiring, the tour was immensely gratifying. The team had been more integrated than on previous tours and although our batting hadn't realised its potential and we were unlucky with injuries, we had regained a large measure of respectability after some lean performances. Mohsin and Mudassar maintained their improvement in subsequent Tests against India and Australia, while Adbul Qadir dominated the Australians with some great bowling. Zaheer and Javed were inconsistent against England, throwing their wickets away in circumstances where their experience should have counted; at Lord's, Zaheer never looked like getting out until he missed a straight one, while Javed was run out in two of his first three innings, with the other an overconfident assault on Hemmings that went wrong. After two series in England, his highest score remains 54, and that's not good enough for a player of his class.

I was happy that my form did not suffer from the burdens of captaincy. Many made comparisons between Ian Botham and me and analysed how the captaincy had affected us in drastically different ways. As I said earlier captaincy is a matter of temperament and ability to understand individuals. Unlike Botham's experience the extra responsibility helped my batting and I hope that it will do so in the future. I still wince at the amount of times I've thrown my wicket away, and I now talk to myself at the crease constantly, drumming home the importance of patience and the needs of my side. But as far as individual comparisons are concerned I find such comparisons pointless unless both players are in the same team: Hadlee and Sarfraz will always be compared unfavourably to Botham because they bowl on unresponsive wickets and have played less Test cricket. I wonder if Botham would ever have bowled much if he'd played for the West Indies? Probably not — he'd have been a batsman. It all depends on the availability of resources and it's silly to make statistical comparisons. My bowling stood up well; I bowled more overs than anyone else on either side, taking 21 wickets in three Tests and although some critics reckoned I over-bowled myself, they should have seen the times when earlier captains had bowled me into the ground. It was certainly difficult for a fast bowler/all-rounder like me to maintain full fitness without sacrificing my batting — fast bowling is a full-time thing that has to be worked at, so I had to devote about ninety per cent of my time to bowling and keeping fit, while just ten per cent was left over to batting. Something had to suffer and it's certainly easier for an all-rounder who bowls medium pace like Ian Botham. It's not often realised how much work goes into bowling consistently fast at the highest level over a period of years. On the 1982 tour, I was dogged by my thigh injury in the first two Tests and when I pulled a stomach muscle two days before the final Test, the physio said I couldn't play for ten days. I decided to take pain-killers and bowl through the injury. Amid the tension of Leeds I forgot about it and luckily I didn't aggravate it. The risk of injury is always there and we have got to get used to bowling through the pain barrier; I think that if I waited until I had no niggles, aches and pains I would probably never bowl!

I went through that pain barrier once too often in the Indian series after the England tour. By the third Test, I could feel a severe pain in my left shin. On the flat wickets, I had to put everything into my bowling, with the result that I made the injury worse. By the fourth Test, it was unbearable without pain-killers and I got through the last two Tests on sheer willpower. I knew something was seriously wrong and eventually it was diagnosed as a stress fracture of the shin. I ought to have had it X-rayed earlier, but foolishly I kept going. The specialist who examined me back in England said it was the second worst injury of its type among sportsmen he had seen and that I might have been finished as a bowler if I'd left it any longer. So a prolonged period of rest was ordered to get me fit for the World Cup.

Despite my shin trouble, I bowled the best of my career in that Indian series (especially in the first four Tests), taking forty wickets. Everything I had learned fell into place, so that I knew what I wanted to do with the ball. I wish I could have done the same in the England series. At the end of the Indian series, I had created a record by taking 88 Test wickets in the year that had just ended. It will surprise many good judges that the best batsman I had bowled at during the year was India's Mohinder Amaranath. At the age of thirty-two, he'd fought back after several years in the wilderness and he batted magnificently in a beaten side against us.

So the captaincy has gone well so far for the compromise choice. Yet I have no illusions at all about the job — one bad season and I'll be out. I just hope that I'll be able to hand over before I get the sack, that I won't have to be told that I can no longer inspire the players. A man like Zaheer, with his vast experience, knows when he's made a mistake and his own fierce pride keeps him up to the mark, while Mohsin needs to be reminded about the need to play his shots with safety. There are no hard and fast rules, although I make a point of acknowledging my tactical errors on the field. I've felt no real pressure so far — apart from the problem of fatigue and of acclimatisation for the home series against Australia straight after the England tour. What I want from the team as captain is that they all give their best: it then doesn't matter if they lose. I got that support on the England tour, when we fielded in the last innings at Leeds, everyone gave their all and defeat didn't hurt me so much. I am annoyed when I know we can do better, for example, with our unpredictable batting. If we try our hardest yet are beaten by a better side, I am the first to congratulate my opponents. The real test for me will come when my form with the bat declines, or I have a spell when I can't take wickets. Team spirit will be tested then. For the moment we have a good, experienced side, although we do lack depth. We have hardly any reserves of quality: Wasim Bari and Sarfraz are past their best, but they still get picked because there are no outstanding challengers. It's a situation that worries me, despite the soaring optimism in Pakistan, where reactions to both victory and defeat tend to be far too extreme. For the moment, I'm grateful for the chance of helping in some of those recent victories, even though I am worried about the state of our cricket.

11 The Future for Pakistan Cricket

In my opinion the standard of first-class cricket in Pakistan is the lowest in the world and if we don't make some drastic changes quickly, we are in danger of becoming the weakest cricket-playing nation within the next ten years.

Most of Pakistan's good Test cricketers are products not of our domestic cricket but of English county cricket. The reason Pakistan became a world-class cricket team in the 70s was because of players like Majid, Asif, Zaheer, Mushtaq, Intikhab, Sarfraz, Sadiq, Javed Miandad and myself. All these players got a chance to play English county cricket and that is what made them world class. It was only because I got into Worcester and Oxford, that I was able to improve my cricket. If I had come back to Pakistan after the 1971 tour I doubt very much whether I would have improved. Most of the above-mentioned players have finished playing and it looks as if no more young Pakistanis will get a chance to play county cricket, so we will have to rely on our own cricket to produce world-class players. Pakistan's earlier cricketers like Moqsood, Fazal, Kardar, Amir Elahi, and Imtiaz were also products of another cricketing system, i.e. of the pre-Partition era when cricket was played on a pentangular system. Our own domestic cricket has produced very few world-class players, Wasim Bari and Hanif possibly being the exceptions. It is sad that the amount of talent this country possesses has never been fully realised. Players like Shafqat Rana, Farooq Hamid, Talat Ali, and many others were extremely talented but faded away because of the dismal standard of cricket to which they were exposed.

Pakistan's cricket is concentrated in the two major cities of Karachi and Lahore. Since eighty per cent of our population resides in rural areas, this means that they are immediately excluded. We are forced to rely on these two cities to produce Test cricketers. I believe that a great deal of talent lies away from the cities. I think that the only way Pakistan can produce fast bowlers is by spotting talent in the rural areas because that is where the strong, healthy young boys live. It is in the villages of the Punjab and the North West Frontier Province that our fast bowling strength lies both physically and temperamentally. It is very important for us to spread cricket throughout Pakistan and the biggest obstacles to this development are the commercial organisations.

Pakistan is the only country in the world where cricket is played between commercial organisations and not between regions, zones, cities or states. The result, I'm afraid, is abysmal. Cricket benefits only in the short run as players are provided with employment, but in the long run we are doing more harm than good. The commercial organisations merely poach players from the regional divisions of Karachi and Lahore, rather than in looking for talent. The result is that the organisations have fifteen to twenty players, whereas the cities or zones have to make teams from what is left.

There is an extraordinary amount of talent in ball games in Pakistan — there are no more than forty squash courts in the whole country, yet our players are the best in the world. The same applies to hockey and to cricket: when I play in club games at home, I see young batsmen playing some remarkable shots that stem from natural ability, far more impressive than their counterparts in England. Yet all that brilliant, precocious talent is largely wasted if it can't flourish in a coherent framework, within which these gifted players can learn how to cope with the tensions and develop their technique for top level cricket.

A city like Karachi that has six million people has no ground of its own. The commercial organisations do not have their own grounds either. This is unique because all other first-class teams in the world have their own grounds. The wickets in Pakistan do nothing at all to help the development of highly talented cricketers. Too much cricket is played on too few grounds, and as a result the pitches are worn out by overuse. They are flat and slow and the imbalance between bat and ball is vast. You only have to take one look at the wicket to be able to forecast a match where hundreds of runs will be scored, the bowlers hardly ever beat the bat and a one-sided contest the inevitable outcome. On occasions, they are under-prepared to help spinners, but for the most part, they are a dream for batsmen. As a result, many artificial records in batting are set up in Pakistan, which look good in the record books but bear little relevance to the way cricket should be played. The dreadful standard of wickets in Pakistan is one reason why we don't produce enough fast bowlers. Unlike places such as Barbados, there is no tradition of fast bowling; batsmen are idolised in Pakistan for their towering achievements. In the West Indies, the wickets are also slow, but they are a naturally athletic, lithe race, beautifully built to bowl fast. Temperament is also a factor: a meek fast bowler is almost a contradiction in terms, and our aggressive types generally come from the north of Pakistan — as in the case of my family. The same applies to fast bowlers from India, the best example being Kapil Dev. The matting wickets of Karachi are also hopeless for a fast bowler: I've played in games there when the spinners have opened the bowling. The soil is very sandy in Karachi and it would simply cost too much to make many turf wickets. Sixty per cent of our Test cricketers come from Karachi and therefore more than half our players are fundamentally ill-equipped to bowl fast.

All the first-class grounds, apart from Lahore and Karachi Stadiums, are neglected; the wickets are badly prepared, the grass is badly tended, the outfields are bumpy, sight screens are often absent, dressing-room facilities are a disgrace and equipment required to produce wickets is absent. Spectator support for first-class cricket is sadly lacking and understandably so. Why should anyone watch a National Bank *vs* United Bank game? There is no loyalty or application involved: players often outnumber spectators, and a great source of potential revenue is lost. If cricket was organised on a regional basis, spectators would be involved, support for their city or state would revive, crowds would flock to games and the money raised could be invested back into the region to develop cricket. Imagine the kinds of crowds at a Karachi/Lahore match: if the grounds and wickets were given to the regions the standard of wickets and grounds would greatly improve. Cricket organised on a regional basis would restore the competitive element that is sadly lacking in our cricketing structure. Regions would be under great pressure from their supporters to pick the best side possible and teams would be chosen on merit alone.

At present, with the commercial organisations in charge, nepotism and favouritism are rampant since they are not under any pressure from their supporters or members. Many talented cricketers suffer because of this. Corruption and nepotism are common in team selection — and I admit I was lucky to benefit initially from nepotism. The experience of Talet Ali is an instructive example. He toured New Zealand with us in 1979 and looked promising, playing a couple of good innings against Richard Hadlee on testing wickets. He was dropped for the Australian tour and then wasn't called to the training camp for consideration for the 1979 World Cup, because he was deemed to be too old at twenty-nine.

Then he was dropped by his club, PIA, from the squad for the next first-class season, because he had no chance of playing for Pakistan again. It didn't seem to matter that in his last match for PIA he scored a hundred and a double hundred! No reason was given and his place was taken by the son of the PIA selector. I don't blame the selector but the system that allows him to get away with this. Talat Ali couldn't leave the airline to play for someone else, because that would mean losing his job; so he stuck at his sales promotion job with PIA and retired from first-class cricket when in his prime. With competition so poor in Pakistan cricket, the strong PIA team will continue to win trophies and no one will ask about poor Talat Ali. All that investment involved in taking him on three Test tours was wasted, as he was ditched at the age of just twenty-nine. In a normal first-class structure, PIA would not have been allowed to get away with such treatment of a player — in England the club is accountable to its members and supporters. No so in Pakistan. Too much is at the whim of powerful individuals.

Due to the absence of properly organised cricket in Pakistan, there have been some very strange selections for the Test team in my time. In 1972, Ehtesham-ud-Din was at his best as a seam bowler and a certainty for the Australian tour: he had taken many wickets at home, as well as seven in the trial match. He was left behind because it was felt that he was unfit. It made no difference that each season he consistently took many wickets for National Bank, or that he specialised in long bowling spells — what was more important was that the portly fellow *looked* unfit. Someone who looked fitter but wasn't in his class as a bowler was taken to Australia instead, with predictably sad results. In doing so, the selectors discredited their own first-class cricket.

In 1979, Talat Mirza was taken to India in case any of our middle order batsmen failed. He was picked on the strength of just a couple of fifties in the handful of first-class games he had played. Shafiq Ahmad was also ignored, even though he has been the most consistent run-getter in our first-class cricket for the last decade. It was said that he lacked he right temperament, but he never got the extended run in the Test side that every batsman needs. Unfortunately, none of the Pakistan captains of that time played much domestic first-class cricket, so they couldn't assess the quality of the home-based players. If Mushtaq and Asif had witnessed any of Shafiq's long, grinding innings on slow turners, they would have seen that he was a master in Pakistan and worth a place on wickets in West Indies, India and England, where the ball invariably keeps low. He could have been our equivalent of Geoff Boycott — solid, reliable and likely to hold things together as the stroke-makers got themselves out.

I realise that the regional sides, apart from Karachi and Lahore, would be very weak but if we encouraged top players to play for the weaker zones, the standard would invariably rise as in Australia where Queensland has outsiders like Chappell, Border and Thomson. Players who could not get into the Karachi side could move to another region. Financial support from local sources could also encourage cricketers. In the long run, Pakistan cricket would improve greatly. The regional associations would set up nurseries to develop and spot young talent; what incentive do they have at the moment to invest in a youngster if he is picked up by a commercial organisation when he is sixteen or seventeen? The regional associations could also reorganise club cricket, bringing them under their own scrutiny, and club cricket could become the basis for choosing first-class teams. Club cricket is played on cement and matting pitches. These surfaces need to be replaced by good, hard turf wickets that would encourage strokeplay, fast bowling and improve cricketing techniques. You cannot produce world-class cricketers on cement pitches. Again the regional associations could invest in wickets and give financial support to clubs. Commercial organisations could have a one-day tournament but they must play a subordinate role in organising cricket; the regional associations must take precedence in organising not only domestic cricket but also matches against touring teams. It is disgraceful that when a touring team plays in Bahwalpur almost all the players are from either Karachi or Lahore. How is cricket supposed to develop in that area? What incentive is there for the youngsters of that area to take up cricket? Clive Lloyd was surprised and commented about this ridiculous method of choosing cricket teams that played against the West Indies. Similarly when Test matches are played in a particular city or state, that city should be responsible for organising it and also for reinvesting the profits in the area. What happens at present is that most of the profit accumulated by local cricket associations isn't accounted for and no one seems to take any interest in finding out where the money goes.

Pakistan's present domestic cricket seems to serve no purpose whatsoever. Apart from the lack of spectator interest, many of the matches appear to be meaningless and a little insignificant. A year ago a team was actually altered at lunchtime in a first-class match in Pakistan. It was a game between National Bank and Pindi and one of the sides had misread the wicket — they got away with drafting in a more suitable bowler after one session of play! In another first-class game in the same period, one team was negotiating a sum of money with the opposition to lose the match when rain washed out the game; one of the sides faced relegation and was working out a deal to let them win. The fact that rain thwarted the plan doesn't alter my view that such an action makes first-class cricket in Pakistan look a complete joke. There are many instances of deserving players, whose performances at first-class level have not impressed anyone. Over the last decade, Pakistan has become the laughing stock of the cricketing world with its regular breaking of established world records achieved against pitifully weak cricket teams. Players like Aslam Ali and Wahid Mirza are the proud holders of world records but none of them have ever been considered good enough to have been included in the Test squad.

Until recently, Pakistan has not played enough Test cricket to be familiar with the highly-charged pressures: in contrast India's Kapil Dev has played as many Tests as me, yet he made his debut seven years after I first played for Pakistan. There is a fine balance to be struck between too much Test cricket and too little, but with our structure so poor at home, we need to get used to the highest form of competition. I believe that if we had played as many Tests in the seventies as the major countries, then we would have fared better, because we would have been more experienced. Playing cricket at the highest level isn't just about physical prowess but you have to learn to cope with crises and situations where nerve and courage are crucial. Such things aren't acquired by grinding down third-rate bowlers on lifeless wickets during matches that are a mockery of first-class status. The higher the quality of the first-class game, the easier it is to attune oneself psychologically to the rigours of Tests.

With English cricket now starting to restrict the amount of overseas players in county cricket, it looks as if the supply of experienced cricketers to the Pakistan Test side is at last drying up. When Zaheer, Javed and myself leave county cricket in the next few years, there will be no Pakistanis left to develop their skills and harden their temperament in a tough, competitive area of top-class cricket. The startling way Majid declined after leaving Glamorgan in 1977 is a chilling reminder of how much we owe to English county cricket when we examine our performances in Test cricket in the last decade. I fear that the outlook for Pakistan is bleak: we will continue to do well in Test series at home, because we'll get by on natural talent and wickets that favour us. When we tour abroad, it will be a different story. We will inherit the results of an appallingly chaotic first-class structure, the desire of English county cricket to look after its own players, the lack of decent groundsmanship and our inability to turn out fast bowlers. Our cricket officials and fans are in a false sense of security at the moment, because we are doing so well. Since 1970, the various Cricket Boards have taken credit for good performances by the national teams, without realising that it had nothing to do with their own domestic cricket at all. Soon we will be back to the sackcloth and ashes or avoidable defeats in Test series, yet if the Board would only sanction a radical shake-up of our system, we could profit from the huge natural talent at our disposal. Unfortunately the Board's reaction to constructive criticism has never been all that impressive: I suspect the players will continue to take all the blame when we lose and politics, wine and women will again be the alleged reasons for our failures. It's much more convenient to invent controversies than concentrate on the desperate need for a revision of our cricket structure.

12   An Outsider's View of English Cricket

There is much to admire about English cricket. I believe it is still the most professionally organised structure in the world. County cricket is a great breeding-ground for anyone who desires to improve his game; in other countries you have to wait for days before you get another chance to make up for mistakes, but in England that opportunity comes along almost every day for over four months. One-day cricket has been a marvellous boost to the finances of county clubs, while bringing cricket to a wider audience and it has also sharpened up fielding standards considerably and made both batsmen and bowlers re-assess how they should play as well as improving running between the wickets. It's good to have a local team to support; members can relate to players they know personally and the team enjoys the feeling of a loyal following that has the interest of that particular side at heart. The high standard of cricket journalism and the excellence of TV coverage also helps to foster interest in the game, and the growth of sponsorship has meant a more realistic attitude to paying cricketers a wage that they deserve. I only wish the many good things about English cricket could be grafted onto the Pakistan version. English cricketers don't realise how lucky they are to play in such a system.

Despite its many and varied assets, the English system fosters mediocrity which, in the long run, is bad for the country's international aspirations. Test matches aren't won by bowlers who bowl accurate medium pace or flat off-spin and compile laborious innings off the front foot. England's team is always difficult to beat, but invariably mediocre, with few attacking players in the side who can win a game by flair. This is partly due to overkill: there is too much first-class cricket in England. Now this may sound strange from someone who bitterly criticises the haphazard Pakistan system, but in England the players get stale through too much cricket — four competitions simply take their toll. It's crazy to expect a county cricketer to drive 150 miles after a game's end to another venue, where he's expected to function at full throttle on the following morning — for a fast bowler, it's a farce. For example, during the days in the seventies when Sussex had a team van driven by a couple of junior players there was an occasion when Paul Parker and John Spencer had to drive at the end of a game from Eastbourne to Leeds. They left Eastbourne at about seven in the evening and got to Leeds at almost 4 am. We were due to start the game at 11 am. If there was a total of sixteen games, each of four days duration, the competition would be keener, because the players would be fresher. There would be more results, because the players would play more positively. Attacking bowlers would be encouraged; at the moment, no county will take a chance on Abdul Qadir, but he would be a match winner in four-day cricket, because he can bowl sides out. The alternative is being out in the field for almost two days, if you rely on the old formula of tight bowling that never troubles good batsmen. The obsession with line and length that dogged my footsteps at Worcester in my early days would be just a waste of time in four-day cricket, because class batsmen would just stay there and accumulate stacks of runs. Fast bowlers and wrist spinners would become crucial ingredients in a captain's plan. The wickets should also be covered; I can see no art in bowling out a side on a wet wicket, it gives an unfair advantage at times to inferior sides. The traditionalists in England say that a 'sticky wicket' is part of the history of the game, but I see nothing admirable about getting hit in the face by a ball that rears up off a length — that isn't good bowling. Good bowling on good wickets that wins matches is the ideal cricket formula for me.

The wickets are too slow in English first-class cricket. I have been lucky to play on good wickets in my county career both at Worcester and at Hove. The Hove wicket in particular rewards the strokemaker and the attacking bowler, because it has bounce — you can play your shots and the edge will carry to the close fielder to reward the bowler who deserves a wicket. If we had played our Tests at Hove in 1982, Abdul Qadir would have picked up many wickets; it was galling to see him baffle all the English batsmen, yet he was thwarted by the slow pitches. David Gower is the most talented English batsman of his generation, but he will always fare better abroad, because he times the ball so well on fast surfaces; lesser players rely on brute strength to punch the ball on slow wickets while Gower's footwork lets him down a little as the ball seams around. If he played regularly on better pitches, he would be even more impressive. The amount of first-class cricket makes it difficult for fast bowlers to keep going. This year Sussex, for example, between the end of May and the end of June, are playing thirty-five days of consecutive cricket. Add travelling to this and what fast bowler can maintain his edge? The fact that Bob Willis is still the best remains an indictment of the system — it's been proved time and again in the last decade that fast bowling invariably wins Tests, but England seems to set its face against the trend. The strange regulations on the over-rate don't help: I agree that a rate must be set, but nineteen an hour is ludicrous. I saw a young English fast bowler sacrificed on the altar of the over rate recently — Paul Newman of Derbyshire was running in from a long way, but he was trying to sort out his rhythm, something that is vital to any fast bowler. He was also trying to bowl fast, not just pitch it on a length. He was eventually taken off because his overs were lasting too long and the captain was worried about a fine for a slow over rate at the end of the season. How will he learn to bowl fast when he can't work at his run-up? If nineteen overs an hour applied to Tests involving the West Indies, they'd be wrapping the games up in three days! Surely the public wants quality, not quantity, a genuine fast bowler provides enough quality to make people forget about over rates. A reasonable over rate would be 15 per hour. The rule about just one bouncer an over in county cricket is equally farcical. It encourages the mediocre batsmen to get on the front foot, knowing he won't get too much flying around his head. How can that regulation help England's batsmen? It doesn't give them any experience in learning how to cope with short-pitched bowling; in Test cricket no reputable fast bowler has any qualms about bowling bouncers if he thinks it will get wickets and he is not hampered by petty restrictions. Bob Willis made that very point when his England team returned from Australia: Willis said the 'one bouncer per over' rule should go, because English batsmen were no longer used to bouncers.

The English game seems to be riddled with anomalies, resulting in confusion and frustration to spectators and players alike. Umpires already have too much on their plates without worrying about the bouncer restrictions. A bad umpiring interpretation of an ambiguous rule led me into a fierce row on the field with Mike Brearley in 1980. It was during a Benson and Hedges Cup quarter final at Lord's, a tense match where tempers were running high. Wayne Daniel had broken a bone in the wrist of Kepler Wessels and although he had been bowling short, Wessels was at least an opening batsman and able to look after himself. I took a different view when Daniel started to bounce consistently Tony Pigott, a tail-ender who couldn't cope. I was batting at the other end and getting more and more angry, because the umpire Jack Van Geloven in their innings had been very strict with wides and bouncers with me. A couple of times, he called wides to my bowling when the batsmen simply played and missed.

I protested to Van Geloven about Daniel's bowling and asked for a ruling; straight away Van Geloven called a wide for one of Daniel's short-pitched deliveries to Pigott. Mike Brearley spotted that the umpire was confused and came running up to me, rather than the umpire. We had a fairly rude exchange of words and Mike Gatting had to drag Brearley away. I was surprised at Brearley, but there were no hard feelings afterwards. Van Geloven later remarked that he'd never heard such bad language before on the cricket field, which was nonsense — we'd all heard a lot worse. I believe he should have been more concerned about the short-pitched deliveries from fast bowlers on either side.

There seems to be a feeling in the English game that every player should be treated in the same way, otherwise team spirit will suffer. I was very near to leaving Sussex in 1981 because of that. I was fined £400 for arriving back two days later than I was supposed to for pre-season training; the club said that the rules applied to all players, but to me that seemed ridiculous. I had been playing all winter and knew that I was fully fit. I stayed in my flat for two days and thought over my future — I could have returned to Pakistan and never played county cricket again. Fortunately, my other Sussex colleagues talked me round, and I'm glad I stayed. It was so illogical, all the other overseas players came back later than me and they weren't fined. The club felt that I was just the same as anybody else on the books, but cricket is not like that; some hadn't been playing abroad and so they needed harder pre-season work than I did. Cricketers should never be categorised in the same way, because one player's value is different from another. The club was treating me like a schoolboy, implying that my experience of twelve years in first-class cricket was irrelevant and therefore my value was no different to that of a youngster who'd just come on the Sussex staff. It hurt my pride.

The English game seems short of genuine enthusiasts on the field. With so much cricket being played in the season, the English player knows he can always make amends the next day. He's just not hungry enough for success, he needs to be more aggressive. The relaxed attitude of the players seeps through to the public, who like an edge to the cricket and can sense a lack of excitement. The same applies to the captains; in my time in county cricket I have only been impressed by Barclay, Brearley and Fletcher among English captains, compared with dynamic South Africans like Greig, Barlow, Rice and Procter. Their English counterparts always appear loathe to take chances; it seems more important to avoid losing money at the end of the season for a slow over-rate than it is to use imagination in playing challenging cricket and gambling for a win. I was amazed when there was such a sharp reaction to our appealing on the 1982 tour to England. That Pakistan team was bubbling over with pleasure at playing Tests again in England — some of us hadn't done so since 1974. We were bound to let off steam occasionally in the heat of the moment. At least we communicated our enthusiasm to the public who came in large numbers to watch us, in contrast to the Indians early in the summer. Javed Miandad irritates some English players because he's verbally aggressive on the field and yet he can relate to the spectators, he's not timid and alienated like many Pakistanis living in England, he's a positive person who won't be dominated. In other words, a personality. He's also a brilliant player and the combination of genius and individuality of mind seems to bother the conservative element in the Establishment, yet is enjoyed by the spectators which is what the game is all about.

This lack of personalities in English cricket seems part of an unconscious desire to have every cricketer playing the same, over-coached way and behaving in the same fashion. Characters can't flourish too readily in English cricket and I admire Ian Botham for getting to the top, while still remaining true to his individualistic instincts. I played against him as long ago as 1974 when I was at Oxford and I was impressed even then by his fighting spirit and aggression. He'll always take the challenge — he's the hardest hitter I've seen and is a vicious destroyer of spin and medium pace. He's probably vulnerable against fast bowling because he takes up the challenge and gives the bowler a chance. He's a dynamic cricketer; he attacks in his bowling as well, giving the batsman a chance by pitching it up and trying to experiment. I've always thought him a very fine bowler in England, where he swings the ball and hits the seam. Abroad, he looks relatively ineffective and unlikely to go through many good batting sides on easy-paced wickets, because the ball doesn't seam around all that much. He has become more open-chested in his action in recent years, which hasn't helped his ability to swing the ball late. Although he's supposed to have a bad back, I don't believe his action has deteriorated because of that. His main problem is that he's overweight.

Geoffrey Boycott is one English batsman I have admired greatly over the years and I wish Pakistan had a few like him to build an innings of 500 round one solid opener. As a fast bowler, I know how vital it is to have someone who can hold up an end at the start of an innings, to blunt the new ball attack and pave the way for the stroke-players. Boycott is a true professional who has worked very hard at his batting and overall fitness. I never entirely agreed with Tony Greig's suggestion that Boycott didn't fancy fast bowling and I was particularly impressed by the way he battled through against the West Indies fast bowlers in 1980 to 81; that took guts, technique and nerve.

Every team needs a Boycott to give the batting stability. County cricket remains the best place to polish talent yet England aren't successful at International level because there just isn't enough natural ability available — something admitted by Bob Willis when the Australian tour ended. Overseas players are used as the scapegoat but this just isn't fair. If anyone says that the standard of county cricket hasn't gone up because of overseas players, then why have Yorkshire won nothing since 1969? They are the only county to have rejected overseas cricketers, yet since the restrictions were eased in 1968, every other county has won a trophy. The quality of play has undoubtedly improved since that time.

I cannot understand why there is so much hostility to overseas players. In 1978, at the height of the Packer Affair, I attended a meeting of the Cricketers' Association to hear sixty per cent of those present vote that English cricket would be better off without overseas players. I was amazed at their attitude, and haven't been to an Association meeting since. I agree there should be no more than two overseas players per side but surely two cricketers per team can't harm English cricket that drastically? World-class players in county sides can only help to raise the overall standard and I wish there was a similar set-up in my country. If you can't produce good English cricketers from the nine remaining places, it's ludicrous to blame overseas players. Shouldn't the critics look elsewhere and wonder why talented sportsmen go to other sports, like soccer? There just isn't enough money in county cricket, its championship structure is too dull and plentiful to attract and inspire younger supporters. One-day cricket is an honourable exception. Generally the English first-class game is not sold enough to the public, compared with tennis, golf or soccer, and it just doesn't appeal to the right age groups. As a result, the present system in

England isn't conducive to creating the best International side in the world.

The other problem with English cricket is the strange selection of the Test teams. For example last winter Gatting was not taken to Australia. He was one of the best English players of my bowling last summer. He has got the technique and guts. Surely he would have coped better on the bouncy, non-seaming Australian wickets than a lot of the English team? Teddy Thomas of Surrey was certainly one I would have taken a risk with. He is possibly the fastest Englishman in county cricket. Being a left armer would also have given the English attack variety — which it sadly lacked and they were over-flowing with medium pacers on wickets unsuitable for them.

13   The Sussex Years

Not once have I regretted my move from Worcester to Sussex. I have had my ups and downs with the Club but, thanks to the team itself, playing for Sussex has been a lot of fun.

I don't recall much about my cricketing activity in my first season for my new county as I was banned for most of the time due to my leaving Worcester. There was however a lot of excitement owing to the Packer controversy.

My first full season started on a bad note. To begin with Arnold Long was made the captain. This I think was a big mistake by Sussex. Though an extremely likeable man with a high moral standard, he was completely unsuitable for the job, especially with a team like Sussex. He was too inflexible about his cricketing views and hated taking risks of any type. His basic philosophy of the game was to make sure the team didn't lose, hence missing out on a lot of opportunities where with a little risk we might have won. He was also scared to get involved in any type of controversy either with the Establishment or the umpires. For instance when Brearley and I exchanged angry words at Lord's, I felt he should have at least had a word with the umpire just to get an interpretation of the rules; Brearley after all went to the protection of W. Daniel when he thought that the umpire wasn't giving him a fair deal. I believe this is very important if the captain wants his team to fight for him. I never had such confidence in A. Long.

The other loss to Sussex was the sacking of John Snow. I

still don't know what the real reasons for this were. He was often accused of not giving his all but I never thought so. Whenever he was needed I felt he gave his best in whatever cricket I played with him. He also provided some great tips to me in the art of fast bowling. I think his critics were unaware of the physical pressure on a fast bowler who plays county and international cricket. Bob Willis, the only other class English fast bowler, hasn't got that hot a record for Warwickshire.

Worse was to follow. Tony Greig, whose dynamic approach to the game was one of the factors for my joining the club, decided that he couldn't play his cricket under Long and left. With Parker at Cambridge, Javed with Pakistan and Keppler doing his military service, Sussex were a pretty depleted team. However, I managed some of my best performances for the Club during this period with both the bat and the ball. By August I had completely exhausted myself and my form deteriorated.

One of the reasons which made me determined to do well in the first half of the season was the poor show put up by the Pakistan team minus the Packer players. We had an incredible match with Gloucestershire, where we bowled them out for a low score and then made over 400 with me getting 167 in a very short time. The fact that this match coincided with the first Test between England and Pakistan is significant. When they batted a second time they were heading for a defeat in two days as I got their first wicket in the first over. Zaheer came in to bat and immediately hit me for a four. Despite my inability to develop aggression against friends and my intense dislike of bowling at them, one four puts an end to any friendship and the desire to avenge the insult takes top priority. Unfortunately for Zed he still thought I was a friend running in to bowl, not even taking any hints from my slightly longer and quicker run, and foolishly wasn't ready for the obvious. He just managed to get a slight touch of his glove on the ball as it hit him just above his forehead. There was a loud crack as he slumped to the ground and the ball ballooned up to Cheatle at gully. I was so concerned about Zaheer's skull that I forgot to appeal and instead rushed to enquire about his health. I might as well have not bothered because he just shook his head and got ready to bat again. Either I had over estimated my pace or his skull was harder than I thought it was. He gave me an accusing look through his glasses and apologising profusely I sheepishly told him that I would give him a single and try to bowl the other player out. I was to regret that decision as he plundered 200 runs off our bowling to save the match for Gloucestershire. In subsequent encounters I was more careful in making such pacts.

At the end of the '78 season everyone got a shock as we won the Gillette Cup. It is significant to note that we almost lost our first match to Minor Counties at Stone while trying to play too safe. Instead of trying to bowl inexperienced batsmen out under pressure Long tried containment with almost disastrous results. It was over this defensive and negative captaincy where we differed so much. I wasn't even allowed to have an attacking field to my satisfaction and found myself playing more the part of a stock bowler than an attacking one.

Long's outlook differed from the rest of the team as well. Most of us had an enthusiastic almost schoolboyish approach to county cricket and the life associated with it; while our captain had played over twenty years of hard county cricket and found our schoolboy pranks rather childish. Once Javed and I played in poor light to win a Sunday League match at Bradford. As we were coming off the field John Spencer and Paul Parker stood on the balcony with torches to show us the way in. We thought it was hilarious but they got a telling off from our captain. It just showed two different attitudes to the game.

It was in fact this light-hearted attitude of the Sussex team that made me enjoy county cricket despite the fatigues and rigours of so much cricket. Players like

Barclay, Spencer, Parker, Mendis, Waller and Javed were always up to some fun on and off the field. This is important when most of the three-day matches at the tail end of the season become meaningless once a team is out of the running for the County Championship.

The '79 season went by without us threatening to win anything even though now and then we could come up with some brilliant performances. In 1980 Sussex signed up Garth le Roux while Javed left to join Glamorgan. He made a great impact straight away. Apart from being a world-class fast bowler, he could get valuable runs in crises and above all was a great team man. I am proud to say that I helped convince him to join Sussex. We had struck up a friendship while playing for the world team in WSC and I knew he would enjoy the enthusiastic and delightful approach of the Sussex team to county cricket. Moreover with the success our partnership had enjoyed with the new ball in WSC we thought we could perhaps help Sussex win the Championship. However we were both in for a rude shock as our captain thought it was too risky to go into a match with both of us as he thought that without Wessels our batting became too weak. In vain I tried to convince him otherwise.

With this 'safe' combination we had a fairly ordinary season until Keppler got injured in June and the 'risky' combination of Garth and I had to be put into operation. From almost the bottom of the table at the beginning of July we reached the number four position in the table by the beginning of August. It was too late to challenge Middlesex or Surrey at the top but we suddenly looked a powerful team.

1981 was the most enjoyable county season I've had and was the most successful for Sussex since I'd joined. To begin with John Barclay was made captain which was the best thing that happened. He was ideal for the team. Apart from being willing to go all out for wins at all costs and leading from the front on the field he also had a remarkable relationship with the team, being able to take jokes even from the junior team members.

The arrival of Ian Gould and the full time availability of Ian Greig also strengthened the team. Indeed they did so well that both represented England within a year. More important was their contribution to the dressing room. While Gould added new dimensions to my knowledge and understanding of Cockney, Greig became the team's news bulletin; you could ask him any gossip about any member on the Sussex staff!

We were devastating. We did well in all competitions and would have won the Championship but for an exceptional season by Notts who did equally well. We suffered somewhat because of an ankle injury to me that kept me from bowling my best for at least six weeks.

We should have beaten Notts in August in what was called by some newspapers the 'Clash of the Titans' but for bad light. We needed one wicket to win the match when play ended. When at the last match of the season Notts beat Glamorgan to win the Championship from us by 2 points we were immensely disappointed, feeling that we were a better team but because of the strange structure of championship cricket we were deprived. Depending on where one's county is located the team can play those counties twice that are either weak or strong. Since the Northern counties in the late '70s have been considerably weaker than the South Eastern ones, Notts were at a great advantage to us.

The disappointment was manifested by the team getting drunk on champagne (luckily I don't drink) and then, led by my friend Garth, streaking round the Hove cricket ground. The next day the club had to face quite a mixed reaction from the residents of the flats that overlooked our ground. Strangely enough some found it rather entertaining.

Sussex now have an excellent team which will be a force in county cricket for the next few years.

14 My Playboy Image

When I read articles in the press about 'Imran the sex symbol', I am frankly amazed. Initially it came as a surprise, because I grew up with a complex about being ugly — fostered by my elder sister who remains astonished to this day to read comments about my alleged good looks. People started to comment on my looks, rather than my cricket from 1976 onwards, as my cricket ability improved; after a time I found it funny and I certainly have never taken it seriously.

I'm not too sure about the advantages of an image such as mine, but I am positive about the disadvantages. Women are constantly wary of me when I first meet them: if I pay someone a compliment it's taken as some sort of devious line that's flung to a million others. The attitude of men is even more disturbing — the ones who feel physically inferior pass remarks on my lack of brains, something of which most sportsmen are accused. Others try to pick fights if they guess that they are stronger than me. As someone who hates violence in all forms, I find such categorisation and instant hostility very disturbing. My advice to all aspiring sex symbols is to make sure they get a double first at Oxford and a black belt at karate!

I've had to live with intrusion into my private life in England since the last Pakistan tour, but it's being going on since 1978 in India and Pakistan. Cricketers are treated like superstars over there, with the best on a par with film stars. When we resumed Test cricket against India in 1978, cricket fever engulfed Pakistan and a whole army of fans was swept along on a tide of passion for a sport they didn't really understand. As a result the press decided to personalise much of the cricket to interest the non-expert: the cult of the cricket personality was born. A year later, the public interest in our tour was even greater in India, surpassing the hysteria in Pakistan; we were virtually prisoners in our hotels as throngs of sightseers and cricket fans waited to see us. I was singled out for much of the attention and consequently the rumours started to flow freely. The fact that we were playing badly and that I was injured helped add fuel to the lurid descriptions. Wild parties, promiscuous Indian actresses and late nights were allegedly my staple diet during that tour; what made such reports so laughable was that I had never been on a tour that was so harshly run by the management. The curfews and fines were so strict that we couldn't have had a wild time even if we wanted to — that tour consisted of nothing but cricket and sitting around listlessly in hotels, with no chance of social diversion. That must have sounded a major disappointment to the sections of the press who were eager for scandal, so they made up a few juicy titbits. I felt some of the scandal-mongers were living out their fantasies through me — attributing to Imran Khan activities they would have indulged in, given the chance. As a captain I believe that disciplinary steps should only be taken against a player when his off the field activities affect his play.

In England, Fleet Street woke up to me as a human being, rather than as a cricketer during our tour in 1982. It didn't seem to matter that I'd played Test cricket since 1971 as the hordes of journalists started writing me up as some sort of playboy figure breezing through the staid world of cricket. Some journalists came to talk cricket with me and went away to print something entirely different, while others said they didn't want to talk about cricket. The result was a succession of ill-informed trash that portrayed me as a kind of dumb sportsman who goes out with dumb blondes, rather than someone who plays a mentally taxing sport to a high degree of professionalism. Many misunderstood why I like to relax away from the pressures of cricket by going to clubs in London with a circle of friends, to talk and relax. I enjoy talking to intelligent people of both sexes and if I'm seen deep in conversation with a pretty girl in a club, the gossip columnists automatically jump to the wrong conclusions, invariably failing to note that I was part of a large circle of friends who were enjoying each other's company. Why should an innocent situation like that be of any interest to the public at large?

I suppose I'm a prime target for the gossip columnists because I'm unmarried and a fast bowler. Fast bowlers have always been the ones to grab the media's attention — I think of Dennis Lillee, Fred Trueman, Jeff Thomson, Keith Miller, Ray Lindwall and, in Pakistan, Fazal Mahmood. We are portrayed as vivid, dramatic characters with a taste for high living and spectacular rows. As a bachelor, the image gets a further polish. In a conservative country like Pakistan, it is considered rare for a man over thirty not to have been a husband and father for several years. I've lost count of the times I've been reported to be married or engaged. Much has been made of the so-called 'clash of cultures' whereby I shall eventually enter into an arranged marriage back home. That represents a choice of systems; I have always intended to live permanently in Pakistan when my career ends and therefore I accept the way it is ordered over there. For the moment, living in England is good for someone like me, who is single and enjoys a private life. That arranged marriage may sound bizarre to many people in England, but it's not all that dictatorial — there is no deadline involved, no need to rush into it.

I have no hard and fast views about marriage, other than the observation that it must be very hard work, whether or not it is arranged. The danger is that because I am thirty, there's likely to be an age gap between me and my bride. I'm very down-to-earth about marriage and rather sceptical of all that 'happy ever after' stuff. I shall follow my instinct about marriage and go into it when the time is right. I would like my wife to be of an independent mind; I relate to people with some depth to them and I want to see my wife using her brains, rather then working in the kitchen. Having grown up with sisters who were pretty independent-minded, I prefer women who are liberated and can think for themselves. I like to think I am a perfectionist — that's why I packed up playing other sports when cricket got hold of me — and I would approach marriage with that same sort of commitment. Greg Chappell has admitted that Test cricket has deprived him of much of the enjoyment of family life, regretting that he missed out on spending enough time with his wife and seeing his two eldest children grow up. That won't happen to me: it's no use having my wife sitting at home while I'm on the other side of the world, playing cricket for up to four months. When I marry, I have to be in a position to spend a lot of time with my wife and family and I couldn't do that while still playing Test cricket. To be a fast bowler who also bats, I have to spend an enormous amount of time getting myself physically prepared: the training and self-discipline that are needed are very time-consuming, far more than for a specialist batsman or a bowler. For the moment, therefore, marriage is out of the question.

The fact that I am shy has been considered to be arrogance, a charge I've had to live with for almost all my life. Now it's true that I was very arrogant as a teenager and young Test player, but I suppose most youngsters who had as protected an upbringing as me would be the same. I like to think I had enough intelligence to realise that life was not going to be always so secure. I am not a naturally confident person; I have gained confidence as I achieved my various cricketing ambitions over the years but before that, I had my various doubts and worries like anyone else. Perhaps I hid them better than others. I'm not an extrovert — I'm shy and reserved in a crowd of people that I do not really know and social relaxation only comes when I'm with a group I know well. Many seem to have preconceived ideas that I'm arrogant and try to be the same right from the start; that has been particularly noticeable in Pakistan, where sometimes the girls decided I was going to be rude and they were determined to fight rudeness with rudeness. As a result, I would react in a way I don't normally.

A section of the Karachi press has always been happy to brand me as an arrogant snob. I have been puzzled by their criticisms and campaigns against me. I can understand that the media builds up a sportsman and when he fails, the criticism is that much more intense. It makes for good reading to see public heroes fall from grace, as Majid Khan, my cousin, discovered during his recent treatment by some of the Karachi press. In my case, I have been roasted without actually failing. I was criticised for my injury on the 1979 to 80 tour of India, which was something I couldn't do anything about and was then aggravated by my enthusiasm to get back into the fray. More recently there were allegations that I had been paid off by the bookies to fake an injury and not play in the World Cup. My selection of Abdul Qadir for the England tour angered some of the Karachi press, even though his quality was obvious and they called it typical favouritism towards a man from Lahore by a Lahore captain, which was ridiculous and proved to be so. I dread to think how Karachi journalists will react to me once I do fail in Test cricket. No doubt I shall experience the same misinformed criticism as when I was pictured manhandling a boy who ran onto the pitch during a Karachi Test. I knew that this boy only indulged in such exhibitions to get himself on television and, unlike some of my colleagues who pat the offender and get the crowd on their side, I wouldn't encourage him. I gripped him very firmly and got him off the pitch, but some Karachi papers completely misunderstood my motives for my action. They said I was being typically arrogant, but I preferred to call it a determination not to have the game taken over by people who can't possibly have the interests of cricket at heart.

Such an insistence on principles has often got me into trouble and caused misunderstandings but I don't see that I should compromise on things that I feel are wrong. As a Moslem, I pray every night for the strength to be honest in life and beg for health and happiness. I have worked hard at my cricket and the success has been doubly satisfying. My concentration on the game in the past few years has been so immense that I have had to discard many of my other interests in life such as shooting, trekking, reading and playing other sports but I know that the much-publicised aspect of my life is drawing to a close. I will remain serious-minded on important issues like South Africa. In 1981, Dr Ali Bacher, the former Springbok captain, offered me a huge amount of money to play in South Africa. He said it was the kind of offer he'd make to Paul Newman — I assume he didn't mean the young Derbyshire fast bowler of that name! I had no qualms about declining to play cricket in a country where a man is considered inferior because of the colour of his skin. That will always remain my viewpoint on South Africa.

On politics, I'm very interested yet remain fairly neutral. I do feel very strongly about underdeveloped countries like India and Pakistan spending a great part of their budgets on defence, when the need to organise their home economies is much more pressing. I am also very concerned that the countries of the Third World are getting poorer with no immediate sign of help.

Issues like South Africa and defence budgets are in the long run far more important than the press cuttings about a man lucky enough to be captain of Pakistan at cricket. Luckily I have always known that images about sportsmen are merely fickle and transient and not to be taken seriously — least of all by the object of such temporary adulation.

Postscript – The 1983 World Cup

I was in a terrible dilemma right up to the start of the World Cup of 1983; should I risk my leg injury by bowling, should I play just as a batsman or should I simply drop out. Dr Peter Speeryn, the specialist who was treating the stress fracture in my left shin bone, told me that the two months rest had led to some healing but the bone was not strong enough to take the full force of my bowling action. He said that there was a serious risk of me opening up the crack if I did take the gamble to bowl, which would put me out of action for the winter Australian tour. The injury had become chronic — I had played for too long with it — and even now I have a race against time to be one hundred per cent fit for the Australian tour. What most people didn't realise was that had I been given permission to bowl by Dr Sperryn it would have taken me at least three weeks to get anywhere near my full pace. My legs weren't strong enough as I had not been allowed to train for the previous two months. So bowling was completely out of the question.

The problem was that never before in my career had I played just as a batsman. Was I good enough to play in the World Cup as Pakistan's number 5 batsman when I had begun to see myself more as a bowler who could bat. Some close friends plus some cricketing friends like Sarfraz advised me to drop out because they thought I was exposing myself to criticism. Without my bowling they didn't think the Pakistan team could live up to the high expectations of our supporters. Finally however I decided to play, partly because I have never been scared of failure and partly because Intikhab Alam thought that my experience of one-day cricket would be useful to the team.

I suppose that at the end of the World Cup after I had topped the Pakistan batting averages I felt relieved that at least I wasn't a liability on the team but I am afraid the frustration I felt at not being able to bowl while we got beaten made me wish I had not played at all. It was particularly galling at Lord's against England and in the Oval semi-final against the West Indies. Both times the wickets were extremely suitable for pace bowling and all I could do was to watch helplessly as we got thrashed. We were without anyone who could get initial breakthroughs or stop the run flow in the final overs. More importantly it was a big blow to the morale of a team that had come to rely on my bowling in the past few years.

There was only one way we were going to win the World Cup and that was if our batting could recapture the brilliance with which India were humbled in Pakistan in the winter of 1982–1983. Unfortunately we put too much pressure on ourselves in trying to cover up for our meagre bowling resources and hence on the whole batted below our full potential.

However in the Oval semi-final against the West Indies I think we batted with a lot of guts and still managed to get 184. We were put in on a damp and uneven wicket against the best pace attack in the world. I doubt if any team could have done much better in those conditions against the West Indies pace bowling. Mohsin's 70 was for me the innings of the World Cup. When they batted we might still have made a game of it if Richards had been caught early-on off Qadir at short leg. Since they depend so much on him they tend to panic if he doesn't score — as they did against India in the final. But it was not to be and Richards after that piece of luck first got himself in and then tore our attack to shreds.

When we were trounced in the semi-finals I was disappointed but did not feel the same frustration I'd felt in the previous two World Cups when I thought we were better equipped to win the Cup. In fact I thought that given our resources we did quite well to even reach the semi-finals.

A lot of criticism for our performance was due to the fact that India won it, with, it was argued, equally limited resources. I must confess that I was one of those who thought that they had no chance having played against their bowling in Pakistan last winter. But in fact it was their bowling that turned out to be their trump card. The bowling that became easy meat on hard wickets became very effective on the soft English wickets. Moreover Binny and Amarnath showed amazing temperament while bowling under pressure. It certainly turned out to be a lot tighter and far more experienced than ours. In the final I thought India virtually threw away the match by some extremely pathetic batting after Mohinder Amarnath and Sirkanth had given them such a marvellous start. They should have got at least 250 if they had batted sensibly. The West Indians then proceeded to put up their worst batting display I have ever witnessed. Richards treated his innings as if it was just an exhibition for the packed Lord's crowd; the target seemed too easy for him to play a proper innings. Once he got out the Indians saw a faint chance and they grabbed it with both hands. The Indian seamers never let the pressure off until the last West Indian wicket fell. It was the same pressure the Indian bowling had applied on England at Old Trafford in the semi-final. Both England and the West Indies had faced relatively less pressure until then — winning most of their matches with comfortable margins.

So I think that rather than condemning us our critics should give credit to India for achieving such a marvellous feat of which no expert of the game thought they were capable.

Index